Hannelore Schmitz

Azores

Translated by Gill Round

40 selected valley and mountain walks
on the nine islands of the Azores

With 78 colour photos and 40 small maps to a scale of 1:50,000

ROTHER · MUNICH

Front cover:
sunny Praia on the east coast of Graciosa.

Frontispiece (photo on page 2):
densely overgrown landscape in the west of Terceira.

All photos by the author except the photos on pages 32, 41, 48 (André Dämmig), 9, 29, 75, 80, 81 (Peter Grimm), title photo, 22, 49 (ICEP – Portuguese Tourist and Trade Office).

Cartography:
walking maps to a scale of 1:50,000,
overview map to a scale of 1:4,000 000
© Freytag & Berndt, Vienna

Translation:
Gill Round

1st edition 2003
© Bergverlag Rother GmbH, Munich

ISBN 3-7633-4818-2

Distributed in Great Britain by Cordee, 3a De Montfort Street, Leicester Great Britain LE1 7HD, www.cordee.co.uk

Preface

Some years ago the Azores were still only known as a feature from the weather map and interest in the unknown archipelago in the Atlantic was gradual. The curiosity of nature lovers who had an interest in exploring was stimulated by the nine islands with sheer coastlines, volcanoes, wind, white beaches, pretty fishing villages and a luxuriant array of flowers.

Many things happen late in the Azores and the search only finally began because Heinrich the Seafarer, the son of a Portuguese king, wanted to get to the bottom of rumours he'd heard about undiscovered islands in the Atlantic. The first islands were discovered just under 500 years ago and Heinrich lent his support to their colonisation. It became lively since there was fighting between the Portuguese and the Spanish for the islands' occupation. Their strategic importance was soon recognised and harbours were built. Settlers had to defend themselves against attacks from pirates and corsairs, but otherwise people lived their own lives on the islands, away from Europe. They learned how to cope with volcanic eruptions and earthquakes; they celebrated religious festivals and peacefully cultivated their fields.

When the first tourists arrived, their interest was concentrated on São Miguel, Faial and Pico. They soon realised that you could go hiking on the islands at any time of the year. The Azoreans were amazed: wasn't it easier to ride on a donkey? And so tourism took off gradually and hiking paths were constructed. Today, the old trading paths which had previously connected one village to another have become overgrown because few people need them any longer or they've been surfaced for use by traffic. And with the help of the EU, which is doing all it can for the Azores, there will soon be even more surfaced roads. So it's not that easy to find suitable terrain for hiking on the islands. But don't let that put you off. There are routes where you are walking on cushions of soft moss and mountain and ridge paths along the caldeiras will obviously not fall victim to tarmac and motorised transport as quickly. Make enquiries about any new hiking paths in the relevant turismo.

The first waymarking of hiking paths, however, has begun. For example on the island of Terceira, the hikers' club is putting up signs for walkers. It's always helpful to have a compass and map, but you can still find your way without a compass if necessary, and friendly farmers will gladly point you in the right direction. On the islands where there's a shortage of public transport, someone will always give you a lift.

Hannelore Schmitz

Contents

Preface 5
General tips 8
The Azores 13
Tourist information 17

São Miguel – something for everyone 22
   Ponta Delgada – the capital of the Azores 26
1 Coastal walk to Mosteros 28
2 From Vista do Rei to Sete Cidades 30
3 From Sete Cidades through the tunnel to Mosteiros 32
4 From Arribanas to Capelas 34
5 From Lombadas to Ribeira Grande 36
6 Over Pico Barrosa, 947m, to Praia 38
7 From Praia to Lagoa do Fogo and back 40
8 From Vila Franca do Campo to 'Nossa Senhora da Paz' chapel . 42
9 Around Lagoa das Furnas 44
10 From Furnas to Lagoa Secca and Pico do Gaspar 46

Santa Maria, the good weather island 50
11 From Santa Bárbara onto Pico Alto 54
12 Stroll to São Lourenço 56
13 From Fonte do Jórdão via Panasco, Piedade
   and Malbusca to Praia 58
14 From Vila do Porto to Praia 60
15 To the 'Nossa Senhora da Fátima' chapel 62

Terceira, the island of contrasts 64
   Angra do Heroísmo 66
16 Stroll up to Monte Brasil 68
17 From Furnas do Enxofre to Algar do Carvão
   and on to Angra do Heroísmo 70

Pico, an island and a mountain 74
18 Ascent of Pico 78
19 From Furna de Frei Matias to Madalena 82
20 Coastal walk to Madalena 84
21 From Miradouro Terra Alta to Prainha 86

São Jorge, the island for hikers 88
22 From Sete Fontes to the Farol de Rosais lighthouse
   and to Rosais 90

23 From Rosais via Serroa to Velas 92
24 Fajã do João Dias and Fajã do Centeio..................... 94
25 From Urzelina to Manadas.................................. 96
26 Over Serra do Topo to Fajã dos Cubres 98
27 From Fajã dos Vimes via Loural to Fajã de São João 102

Faial – hinting at the wider world 104
28 A walk round the caldeira and descent into the crater basin... 106
29 From the caldeira to Horta 108
30 Monte da Guia and Caldeira do Inferno 112
31 From Lombega to Ponta de Castelo Branco
   and to Castelo Branco.................................... 114
32 From Capelo to Capelinhos 116

Graciosa – for walking and relaxing.......................... 118
33 Monte Ajuda... 120
34 Round walk from Santa Cruz via Dores
   and along the coast 122
35 Furna do Enxofre and round the caldeira 124

Flores, the island of flowers 126
36 From Santa Cruz to Ribeira da Badanela 128
37 From Lajedo to Mosteiro 130
38 From Fajãzinha to Fajã Grande........................... 132

Corvo, the smallest of the islands 134
39 From Vila Nova do Corvo to the caldeira 136
40 To the north-east coast of Corvo 138

Index 140

General tips

Use of the guide
The contents page gives an overview of all the suggested walks. The most important information precedes the walk descriptions in dossier-like form. The line of the route is marked on the colour walking maps (scale 1:50,000). The index contains all destinations, locations, starting points and bases as well as the major objectives of each stage. There's also a map showing the location of each walk.

Grade
Most of the walks go along clear paths and tracks. However you should be aware that some of the walks still require fitness, sure-footedness, a lack of vertigo and good route-finding ability. You should also take into consideration the fact that the walks might go up a grade if there's a change in the weather, as can so often happen in the Azores.
To help you assess the level of difficulty, the walk numbers have different colours as follows:

Lava arch on the coast of São Jorge.

Hydrangea hedgerows separate the meadows on São Jorge.

BLUE

These paths are for the most part wide sufficiently and only moderately steep, and therefore relatively safe even in bad weather. They can be undertaken by children and older people.

RED

These mountain paths and tracks are mostly narrow and can be rather exposed for a little way, so they should be undertaken only by sure-footed hikers. Some fairly short sections might require more demanding route-finding.

BLACK

These mountain paths are frequently narrow and steep, very exposed in places and you need to take care over slippery sections. Only very rarely will it be necessary to use your hands. These paths should only be undertaken by sure-footed mountain walkers with good route-finding ability.

Dangers

You are always welcome as a hiker in the Azores. But as the locals are not hikers themselves, you cannot get from them any information about the actual state of the paths or the weather conditions in the mountains etc. So take note of the weather tips given here for individual islands.

When planning your walk you should take into account the frequent change

The 'Nossa Senhora da Fátima' chapel on Santa Maria.

in the Azores weather. There are often sudden gusts of wind which can be dangerous on the rim of a caldeira, for example. These gusts of wind can occur from any direction without warning and cause you to lose your balance. Find something to get hold of, rocks, ferns or heather, or lie down on the ground.

It goes without saying that you should keep your distance form boiling, bubbling sulphur springs like in Furnas, for example.

Best time to travel
The Azores are an excellent destination for your summer travels, since in the winter months you can expect cool weather and heavy rainfall. The best time for travelling and hiking is therefore the months of June to September when you can expect the most settled weather.

Equipment
If you are planning lengthy walks, you will need sturdy footwear with good soles. The paths on São Miguel, São Jorge and Faial can be very slippery after rain. On São Miguel there are also old trading paths with large, smooth stones which are lightly covered in sand. There's the risk of slipping here too. Take a walking pole with you on long walks to lessen the chance of damaging your discs and knees and to give more stability. You should wear hard-wearing trousers, take a sun-hat and sun-cream. A shower-proof

jacket and a pullover are better than an anorak and also it's a good idea to protect your rucksack. You can get soaked through in a heavy downpour in the Azores, and then you will freeze. Take a towel and some spare clothing.

Refreshments

With the exception of Graciosa and Santa Maria the islands are only inhabited on the coast, and so that's where you will find restaurants, generally small and cosy, providing for the locals. In the mountains, on the other hand, there are few places to buy food and to shop so you will need to take your own provisions with you.

Access

Special mention is given to access alternatives in the descriptions of the individual islands since each one of the nine islands is different.

Tips for long-distance walkers

Most of the walks have been conceived as one-way day walks where the destination is a long way from the starting point. If this is the case it is recommended that you travel by bus or taxi.

The bus facilities vary from island to island. On many of the islands the buses are numbered, but on others not marked at all. The best bus network is on São Miguel. Due to the inconsistent bus services, special mention is given to each island's transport.

The austere north coast of São Miguel.

The symmetrical boundaries of Terceira meadows.

Protection of nature and the environment

In principle do not go across cultivated land – agriculture is the most important source of income in the Azores. Leave gates as you found them. Do not pick any fruit – you can buy it cheaply from the farmer or at the market. Do not take any plants away with you. Do not light a fire anywhere except in the barbecues at picnic areas. Do not disturb the animals. The importance of environmental protection has not penetrated every part of the Azores, but do not allow yourself to leave any litter behind. Leave everything just as you found it.

Maps

The maps provided with each walk are an integral part of the guide. Should you require additional maps, have a look at the road map, scale 1:75,000 by Freytag & Berndt, the ten individual maps, scale 1:50,000 from the Instituto Geografico e Cadastral, Ponta Delgada, as well as the 35 (unfortunately rather antiquated) military maps (Carta de Militar de Portugal), scale 1:25,000. The maps can be bought on the spot in Ponta Delgada.

The Azores

Nine very different islands

The Archipelago of the Azores, three groups of islands of volcanic origin, lie in the Atlantic, 760 nautical miles from Lisbon and 2110 nautical miles from New York. Atlantis? No, they are not the remains of this legendary continent, although you still meet researchers of Atlantis on the islands who are looking for new evidence for the old theory. The archipelago got its name from the birds of prey that were indigenous at the time of discovery, as a kind of dedication.

The islands are, geologically speaking, young. The youngest, Pico, is only 200,000 years old and the other eight originated 1 to 5 million years ago. They lie on the Mid-Atlantic Ridge, the largest range of mountains on earth, a plateau rising from a depth of up to 2000m. The location, almost in the middle of the Atlantic, has a determining influence on the weather which can vary greatly from island to island. What is more, each island has its own character – that's what makes travelling and hiking in the Azores so interesting.

The discovery and the history of the islands

Heinrich the Seafarer, Infante Dom Henrique, the second son of the Portuguese king João I, wanted to investigate the rumours concerning unknown islands in the Atlantic. Various Italian maps of the 14th century showed islands in the Atlantic. The Italian Pizigano drew a map of the Atlantic in 1367 with an indication at the place where Corvo lies. But there was no concrete evidence. In 1427, commissioned by Heinrich the Seafarer, Captain Diogo de Silves discovered the island of Santa Maria.

AN OVERVIEW OF THE ISLANDS

The Azores consist of three groups of islands:

Eastern group

Santa Maria (97 sq. km; highest elevation: Pico Alto, 587m; the three uninhabited Formigas to the south of the island)
São Miguel (757 sq. km, the largest island and with about 126.000 inhabitants the most inhabited island of the Azores; highest elevation: Pico da Vara, 1103m)

Central group

Terceira (397 sq. km; highest elevation: Santa Bárbara, 1021m)
Graciosa (61 sq. km; highest elevation: caldeira, 402m)
Faial (172 sq. km; highest elevation: Cabeço Gordo, 1043m)
Pico (483 sq. km; highest elevation of the archipelago: Ponta do Pico, 2351m)
São Jorge (238 sq. km, highest elevation: Pico da Esperança, 1053m)

Western group

Flores (142 sq. km; highest elevation: Morro Alto, 914m)
Corvo (17 sq. km, the smallest island by far; highest elevation: Morro dos Homens, 718m)

13

Introduction

The discovery of the remaining islands happened in quick succession with the exception of Corvo and Flores which were not discovered until 1452. In order to encourage their settlement, Heinrich had cattle released on the islands. The first settlers were the Portuguese, in particular from the Algarve coast, and the Flemish who wanted to escape religious persecution. The strategic location of the islands led to changing claims to power and armed conflict. What is more, the settlers had to defend themselves against pirates and corsairs (north-African pirates). The fortresses remain as evidence of this time.

In 1976, the islands which had belonged to Portugal since their discovery, received the status of an autonomous region with Ponta Delgada as the capital. The ministerial offices are distributed between the islands of São Miguel, Faial and Terceira just like the university faculties.

Flora and fauna

The Azores are a paradise for flower lovers and botanists. There are over 850 flowering species of plants and fern, 56 of them are endemic, i. e. they can only be found in the Azores. Furthermore – and this is really something quite special – you can find 425 species of moss. The Azores are the islands of the hydrangea which has become their symbol and logo. Hydrangea hedgerows adorn the roadside and separate the individual fields from one another. Their delicate blue blossom in June continues to deepen in colour. The azalea blossom already starts in March and lasts until June. Also lilies, orchids and white arum lilies line the roadside. The majority of trees in the villages, at the roadside and in small woods are juniper, laurel, the dragon

ZONES OF VEGETATION

When the first settlers came to the Azores the islands were densely overgrown by forest (mainly laurel woods). In order to make way for grazing land and fields, to build houses and provide fuel, many of the trees were felled. They only remained where access was difficult, as for example in steep-sided gorges. The zones of vegetation can be classified as follows:

0 to 200m

The ground in the coastal regions can be stony, rocky or sandy and consist of volcanic lava. Grass, small shrubs and flowering plants grow here, in some places there are also woods. Most of the settlements are near to the sea and therefore gardens, fields, meadows and vineyards too.

200 to 500m

Predominantly pasture-land, in some places fruit trees have been planted, sometimes evergreen trees too.

500 to 1100m

Evergreen trees, especially laurel, ferns, heather, many kinds of moss, flowers and shrubs which require a high humidity.

Over 1100m

You find this vegetation zone only on Pico. Moss especially grows here, small shrubs, lichen, anything which does not require a lot of moisture.

Luxuriant display of flowers on Santa Maria.

tree, the araukarie, oaks, elms, acacia, plain trees, Japanese cedars and eucalyptus trees. You can buy a book on botany in the Azores in four languages, Açores – Flores by Erik Sjögren, in Ponta Delgada and Horta.

In contrast to the plant world, the animal world has considerably less diversity. 36 species of birds live here, amongst them quails, wood snipes, gulls, gannets and the cagarra (Cory's Shearwater). The latter has disturbed many tourists with its nightly cry of 'aua-aua' from April to June when it's the breeding season. There are also many lizards and rabbits, both of which often find their way into the cooking pot.

Since whale catching has been banned there are possibilities for whale watching, for example on Faial, São Miguel, Pico and Corvo.

There are also the usual pets, large numbers of black and white spotted

15

cows, horses, moles, donkeys, pigs, hens and dogs to guard people's property. Black bulls graze on Terceira which are used at the 'Mascardos da Corda', a lively, bloodless bullfight on a rope.

Weather

There's a saying in the Azores: 'Every day has four seasons.' The weather not only varies from island to island, but also changes during the day.

A mild sea climate, influenced by the Gulf Stream, dominates the islands. The average temperature in winter is 13 °C and in summer 23 °C.

On Santa Maria and Graciosa there's a lot of sunny, dry weather because the wind quickly sweeps the clouds over the low mountains.

They say about Corvo that it rains 300 days in the year.

On São Miguel there can be stormy weather up in the mountains with thick fog and heavy rain showers, while down on the beach you can be soaking up the sun.

The Azores' high pressure, which every European takes for granted, is not absolutely reliable. All you can be sure of are the trade winds which always come from the north-east (June to the beginning of September) and produce fine weather.

On the other hand the wind can get up to force 12 in the 'wind tunnel' between Faial, São Jorge and Pico. At such times the airports (especially in Corvo) remain closed and sailors in the marina are forced to take a break. Because this is not a recent phenomenon, about 500 ships have accumulated on the sea bed between the islands over the years. Ships used to sail between the Azores only with the greatest respect, especially in winter. There's sometimes even a tornado as well, and on the odd occasion a typhoon in winter.

It's important for hikers to look at the weather forecast (on RTP at 21.00 on Azores TV) and out of the window in the morning. You should always keep an eye on the level of the clouds on your walk and be prepared to turn around if there's sudden fog.

In other words, the Azores offer 'a menu of weather' which provides plenty of variety if you're prepared for it.

CLIMATE IN THE AZORES (SÃO MIGUEL)													
Month		1	2	3	4	5	6	7	8	9	10	11	12	Year
Temperature °C		15	15	16	17	18	21	23	24	23	20	18	16	19
Precipitation mm		120	100	105	67	62	42	27	29	81	103	120	102	958

Tourist information

Getting there
All flight connections to the Azores go via Lisbon and require a changeover onto a SATA plane. Flights between the islands can be booked with SATA (in Ponta Delgada, Avenida Infante Dom Henrique, or at the airports on other islands). During a storm the airport is closed depending on the force of the wind, so you might have to alter your travel plans.
There's usually a boat between Horta (Faial) and Madalena (Pico) as well as between Horta and Velas (São Jorge). In summer there's also one between Flores and Corvo.

Shop opening times
Usually from 9.00 – 12.00 and from 14.00 – 18.30, on Saturdays from 9.00 – 13.00. Banks are open Monday to Friday from 8.30 – 14.45. The further you are away from Ponta Delgada or São Miguel, the more likely the variations.

Walking on Terceira.

Festivals
Many lively festivals are celebrated on the islands. A selection of the most important ones are: carnival (especially on Graciosa), Easter Sunday, Festivals of the Holy Spirit (from Easter Sunday to the end of summer), bullfights (on Terceira from May to October), Festival of Christ (São Miguel, 5th Sunday after Easter), Festival of St. George (São Jorge, on the 29th May), Festival of St. John (Terceira, Faial, São Miguel and Flores, on the 24th June), Festival of St Peter (São Miguel, on 29th June), Sea Week (Faial, first Sunday in August), Festival of the Virgin Mary (Corvo, 15th August), 'Cais Agosto' (Pico, first weekend in August), Whalers' Festival (Pico, last weekend in August), Wine Festival (Pico and Santa Maria, first weekend in September).

Crime
There's hardly any crime to speak of. There's no theft on the small islands because there's little chance of the thief escaping. Women need not be afraid to walk on their own in the Azores – it is not in the nature of an Azorean to pester women.

Begging
Sometimes tourists in Ponta Delgada (São Miguel) are accosted by beggars: small boys and elderly women. This should not be encouraged.

Emergency telephone number
115 on all the islands.

Picnic areas
If there is not a festival going on in their village, a favourite pastime of the Azoreans on Sundays and Bank Holidays is to go for a picnic. So, with the exception of Flores and Corvo, you will find picnic areas on the islands with wooden tables, seats and sun-shades made from woven branches. They are usually well-placed for swimming too.

Accommodation
At the present time there are about 5000 beds on the islands which suit all tastes: 4 to 5 star hotels, apartments, guest houses, bed and breakfast places and holiday houses in which you can sometimes also rent single rooms. In high season (end of June to the beginning of September) you should certainly book ahead. There's a shortage of accommodation on both the western islands of Flores and Corvo.

You will find campsites on the islands of São Miguel, Terceira, Pico, São Jorge, Faial and Graciosa – information can be obtained from the regional tourist board. Wild camping is permitted up to a certain point, but you should always obtain permission from the owner of the property first.

A bit at a loss with the menu

If you are expecting a culinary paradise in the Azores you will be disappointed. The local specialities are quite simple and not at all what Europeans are accustomed to as many dishes are served without sauce. There are restaurant owners who have made a note of this and provide visitors from the mainland with ketchup and mayonnaise.

Ralph and Hertha Kunze have brought out an Azorean-German menu which you can obtain from the local tourist office and also in many restaurants free of charge. Of course there's a great variety of fish dishes from red gurnard to barracuda and of seafood from mussels to crabs.

But you should definitely also try the local soups and the various casserole dishes which come closest to mainland tastes. Try as well the many tra-

On Graciosa, farmers still drive donkey-drawn carts.

Waves crashing over the rocks on the north coast of São Jorge.

ditional sweets of the region and, very important, the pineapple from São Miguel and the excellent cheese from the island of São Jorge. The cheese goes very well with the local red wine.

Azorean wines are heavier than the table wines that mainlanders are accustomed to, for example, the aperitif wine from the island of Pico, the wines from Graciosa, Santa Maria and Biscoitos on the island of Terceira. If you prefer a lighter wine, order the crisp Portuguese 'Vinho Verde', available together with other Portuguese wines from the mainland. But there are also other Azorean wines which you should taste, the 'Vinho do Cheiro' and the 'Vinho da Região'. Vinho da Região tastes and smells a bit like strawberries. Don't forget to try the fig schnapps on Pico and the brandy on Graciosa too.

Holiday activities in the Azores

The Azores are ideal islands for hiking. Efforts are being made to way-mark hiking paths, compile maps and publish walking guides.

Cycling is also popular and you can rent a bike on various of the islands.

For those with a special interest there are different geological courses on offer. A variety of interesting botanical courses are available from the island's tourist office, sometimes in conjunction with hikes.

All types of water sport are possible. The island of Faial is well-known for sailing on the open seas and São Miguel is recommended for diving.

Surfers get as good value from the lakes and beaches as swimmers do. Deep sea fishing is becoming more popular and organised whale-watching between April and September is very informative, with 20 species of whale. Speleology is offered on Graciosa and Terceira.

There are three 18-hole golf courses to choose from. You can therefore combine hiking with many other activities.

Language
The official language is Portuguese. But the dialects can vary enormously from island to island. In general, people swallow the end syllables. An example is 'thank you' = 'obregada' (feminine) and 'obregado' (masculine). In the Azores it's simply 'obrega'.

Most people, especially young people on the more popular islands, speak a little English. Those Azoreans who have worked in the USA or Canada have a fair amount of English. You can also get by with French or Spanish. It's interesting to listen when Azoreans who have worked in the USA are conversing in Portuguese. Before they emigrated they didn't know a series of expressions in Portuguese and then they learnt these in English, so that a mixture of Portuguese and English has evolved.

DICTIONARY FOR WALKERS

angra	bay	lagoa	crater lake
areia	sand	lajes	plain
cabeço	hill	levada	canal
caldeira	basin, crater	lomba	mountain ridge
calheta	narrow bay	mata	wood
caminh	path	miradouro	viewpoint
canada	narrow path	misterios	wooded lava
fajã	coastal plain		fields
farol	lighthouse	morro	hill
flores	flowers	paragem	bus stop
furna (do enxofre)	cave (sulphur)	pico	mountain peak
igreja	church	ponta delgada	narrow
ilha	island		promontory
ilhéu	small rocky	porto	harbour
	island	praia	beach
imperio	chapels on	quinta	estate
	Terceira und	ribeira	river
	Faial	rua	road
lactinios	milk collecting	serra	mountain ridge
	point	vale	valley

São Miguel – something for everyone

São Miguel, with its 757 sq. km., is by far the largest of the islands and with 135,000 inhabitants also the most important and touristically speaking, the best developed. However, in spite of this, there are no giant hotels and no tourist rip-offs, even if the prices are a little higher than on the smaller islands. If you are visiting the Azores for the first time you should concentrate on São Miguel. There is so much to see there, you will have no problem in filling a two-week holiday. The people who live on the other smaller and less developed islands look rather enviously on the more attractive main island and would have you believe that the people of São Miguel are greedier and more unfriendly. But it's only a bit of local rivalry, as everyone who comes to the Azores from Europe or the USA lands at Ponta Delgada airport first. It was, by Azorean standards, expanded and improved in 1995.

Many people who go to the Azores for a walking holiday are coastal walkers. In combination with the public bus service, you can go round the island on foot – there was previously a donkey path all round the island – as well as by bike which you can hire in Ponta Delgada.

On the island there are three beautiful recreational centres – for walking, looking round, relaxing and swimming. In the west you will find the caldeira of Sete Cidades interesting, the only intact caldeira in the Azores in which

Caloura on the south coast.

Coastal scenery between Praia and Ribeira Chã.

they built a village. You can even find accommodation there. Further east, almost in the middle of the island, there's the Serra de Agua de Pau with the dark and mysterious crater lake 'Lagoa do Fogo'. The third walking and recreational centre is the Vale da Furnas, a paradise for lovers of wild flowers, with the biggest thermal pool (naturally warm pool) in the world and bubbling sulphur springs.

There are no marked hiking paths, but an effort is being made to expand the network of paths, and up in the mountains, above Lagoa do Fogo, there are already two stones marked with directional arrows and others are to follow.

Although you will not find many sandy beaches on São Miguel it's usually worth taking your swimming things – you will always find a small bay or lake where you can swim. It's an absolute must for you to take swimming things with you in the volcanic region of Furnas.

The eastern side of the island with Serra da Tronqueira, in places over 900m high, is not as developed as the west. The highest mountain on the island is Pico da Vara, 1103m, also in the east.

At Gorreana in the north of the island you can marvel at the tea plantations, something quite rare and unique in Europe. Tea varieties from China and India are cultivated on about 60 hectares of land. The mostly black tea has an excellent taste. The reason for it being little known is due to the fact that the 60 tons approximately harvested each year is drunk by the Azoreans them-

The 'Convento de Nossa Senhora da Esperança' in Ponta Delgada at the Festival of Christ.

selves.

The big pineapple plantations of Fajã de Cima are also a tourist attraction. Excursions are made here from Ponta Delgada. In the shops you can buy anything to do with pineapples in some shape or form.

The drying racks, seen all over São Miguel, are used principally for the drying of tobacco.

The Azorean people are religious and the fear of natural catastrophes has contributed to this. The largest religious festival is the Festival of Christ

(Senhor Santo Cristo do Milagres) which takes place on the 5th weekend after Easter in Ponta Delgada.

Also interesting are the 'riding games' of Ribeira Seca on 29th June, the procession of the Saviour of the Sick in Furnas, the procession of St Michael in Vila do Campo and the festival 'Bom Jesus da Pedra'. During Lent groups of men, each one for eight days, walk to the churches dedicated to the Virgin Mary. On their return a festival is celebrated in their home village in which everyone takes part.

The music of São Miguel is rather melancholy, due in part to the long period of isolation from the outside world. When there's dancing don't miss the 'Sapateia' and 'Manjericão', the 'Pézinho da Vila', the 'Balho Furado' and the 'Cana Verde' dances. There are about 30 bands on São Miguel and they perform mainly in the music pavilions opposite the churches.

A SUMMARY OF INFORMATION ABOUT SÃO MIGUEL

Bus service

In comparison to the other islands the public transport on São Miguel is really good – you just need to get used to it.

The airport lies about 2km from Ponta Delgada town centre. The airport bus goes every hour and you can find out the exact times from the posto turismo at the airport. There are three bus companies on the island and the main bus stops are near the post office on Avenida Infante Dom Henrique in Ponta Delgada. You will also find the turismo here where you can obtain a map of the town, bus time-tables and other information.

The buses to the west leave from the side of the road going towards town, the buses to the east from the side of the road going towards the sea. There are no time-tables at the bus stops and many of the stops are not even marked, as for example, the one from Ribeira Grande towards Ponta Delgada. Since there is hardly anyone who speaks English in Ribeira Grande you should try out a bit of Portuguese – people are very friendly and helpful.

The three bus companies are marked accordingly. 'Viação Micaelense' goes to Sete Cidades and Capelas, so to the west and north-west, 'Varela & Filhos Lda.' to Lagoa, Vila Franca do Campo, Gateira, Furnas and Povoação along the south coast and 'Caetano Raposo & Pereira' covers the route via Ribeira Grande to Furnas. Buses rarely go to Maia and the north east.

You should also be aware that the buses sometimes depart ahead of schedule. If you want to get off at a certain stop ring the bell on the bus to alert the driver. On the road put out your hand if you want the bus to stop at a bus stop or alternatively you can flag down a bus on the open road.

Taxi and hire car

You need to carefully plan one-way walks where public transport is not available. Travel by taxi to the proposed starting point, calculate the walking time (including breaks) and order the taxi for the allotted time at the end of the walk.

The taxi drivers are totally reliable and you will be collected punctually at the end of your walk. Of course, hire cars are best suited for cross-island trips and round walks, but at the present time there are not many of these.

Another possibility is to rent a bike or join an organised bike tour.

São Miguel

Ponta Delgada – the capital of the Azores

Ponta Delgada, which was 450 years old in 1996, was once a sleepy little town. It's now on its way into the future. From its position as the hub of the islands and the continents of Europe and America. There are 40,000 inhabitants and a large part of the university and the ministerial offices are to be found here, the seat of government of the autonomous region of the Azores, an airport which has become quite large, a harbour, into which even trans-Atlantic ships sail, a new marina, large banks and hotels, many restaurants, splendid churches and shops where you can buy absolutely everything. 'It's a bit more expensive,' is what the inhabitants of the other islands say, not without a hint of resentment. For it's widely recognised that Ponta Delgada is the most significant and the biggest town in the Azores, even if it does still reveal its provincial apron strings and is lacking somewhat in comfort. There are hardly any street cafés. People mostly meet up at the harbour wall where the buses stop too. The main street is the Avenida Infante Dom Henrique with the tourist office which should be your first port of call for a town plan, maps, bus time-tables etc. Then there's the post office, several banks, the offices of the TAP and the SATA, a shopping centre and hotels, and lots and lots of traffic.

Go and have a look at the São Bras fort which was built in 1552 as a defence against pirates and is today a garrison, although many would prefer to turn it into a hotel like they've done with the Horta fort on Faial. The most attractive (photo) motif of the town is the city gate on the Largo de Gonçalo Velho Cabral with its three arches and the towering clock tower of Igreja Matriz de São Sebastião, built in Manueline style with a magnificent, opulently gilded, carved altar. The town hall is situated opposite, an Azorean baroque construction from the year 1723. Notice too the pavements – the beautiful mosaic-like design popular almost everywhere in Ponta Delgada and other towns in the Azores, and which can be seen on the mainland and in Madeira as well.

The festival of the 'Senhor Santo Cristo dos Milagres' takes place every year at the beginning of May and even emigrants from the USA and Canada travel over for it. The festival revolves around the extraordinary life-size wooden figure of Christ on the cross, to which there is, of course, a long history. Middle-point of the festival is the Plaça 5 de Outubro with a small music pavilion. The statue of Christ is here in the 'Convento de Nossa Senhora da Esperança' where the procession starts from. On the other side of the square is the S.José church. Both are decorated with pictures on azulejos (blue and white patterned tiles) and paintings. The path of the procession is beautifully laid out with flowers and the church façades, as well as the whole of the square, are trimmed with thousands of lights on feast days. This is where people meet up in the evening. There's music in the pavilion, a carousel for children, ice-cream sellers and families strolling up and down – nothing more. If you're unlucky with the weather you should make a visit to the Carlos Machado museum with many scientific and ethnographic exhibits in a beautiful convent from the 17th century. The little streets and alley ways of Ponta Delgada lead uphill almost parallel from the harbour mole. They are constructed in such a way so that water runs quickly and easily back down again if the waves surge up too far.

The northern part of the town is an exclusive residential quarter with magnificent villas and elegant grounds. There was rivalry amongst the rich people in earlier times, especially with regards to the grounds. The president of the autonomous region of the Azores lives today in the palace of Santa Ana in the Jardim Jacome Correia. If the gates are open you are allowed to go into the park.

It is not attractive around Ponta Delgada with all its factories and unsightly building works. There's no point in walking through these ugly outskirts to find your way out of town and get to the coast or up into the mountains. It's better to take a taxi or use public transport. No Azorean would think of walking up.

The Convento Nossa Senhora at Largo de Camões.

1 Coastal walk to Mosteros

To a picturesque fishing village

Ginetes – Pico das Camarinhas – Ponta do Escalvado – Mosteiros

Starting point: Ginetes, 160m. Bus from Ponta Delgada (bus company Viação Micaelense, No. 8) and Mosteiros.
Destination: Mosteiros, 40m. Bus to Ginetes as well as Ponta Delgada.
Walking times: Ginetes – Pico das Camarinhas ¾ hour, Pico das Camarinhas – Ponta do Escalvado 1 hour, Ponta do Escalvado – Mosteiros 1¼ hours. Total time about 3 hours.
Height difference: 120m in descent.
Grade: easy walk.
Refreshments: restaurants in Mosteiros with fish specialities.
Tip: by starting in Feteiras you can lengthen the walk by 6 hours.

If a look out of the window in the morning tells you that clouds are already forming in the mountains of São Miguel, you are advised to postpone your trip into the mountains to another day when there are no clouds. On those days the sun is usually shining down on the coast and a coastal walk is more appealing. There used to be a donkey path all round the island which connected the villages on the coast. Today it has given way to tarmac roads, but there are still some beautiful stretches which you can use for a coastal walk. A particularly beautiful route goes from Ginetes to Mosteiros in the west of the island. If you walk in this direction rather the reverse, it offers nicer views.

In **Ginetes** go left from the Piazza along an unsurfaced path to a plane tree at the centre of a T-junction. When you go through the village you should notice something special – the old-style ovens built on the outside and the enormous chimneys which you no longer find in other villages. From the junction walk along Rua do Moio until the stables on both sides of the road come to an end and turn left towards a volcanic rock needle, **Pico das Camarinhas**, 219m, which is densely covered in heather. From the top you have a beautiful view of Ponta da Ferraria. Round some hairpin bends you come to a former bathing place for sufferers of rheumatism. Today there are several picnic areas here and hot springs in the sea. Be careful! At low tide they can be very hot. There's a detour along an unsurfaced path to the north over the steep coastline to the beautiful **Ponta do Escalvado Belvedere** viewpoint.

Continuing along the main path again, it turns into a small tarmac road after 2km which you follow over the cliffs. You have a wonderful view of the Ilheu dos Mosteiros, other rock pinnacles rising out of the sea and the fishing village of Mosteiros. You walk away from the coast around a gentle bend and reach the centre of **Mosteiros** where the two roads cross each other at right angles in front of the church and the bus stop. The houses are one storey high and painted shining white. You'll find a lot of grain barns on wooden stilts to protect against the damp and rodents. There are several fish restaurants in the village.

The coast near Moura on the way to Mosteiros.

2 From Vista do Rei to Sete Cidades

Royal view

Vista do Rei – Lagoa Verde – Lagoa Azul – Sete Cidades

Starting point: Vista do Rei, 656m. Bus from Ponta Delgada. Get off the bus at the crater rim at the Miradouro stop and go about 200m east to the famous Vista do Rei viewpoint, 580m.
Destination: Sete Cidades, 256m. Bus to Ponta Delgada.
Walking times: Vista do Rei – tarmac road ¾ hour, detour along Lagoa Verde

40 min., shore path on Lagoa Azul to the picnic area ½ hour, picnic area – Sete Cidades ½ hour. Total time 2½ hours.
Height difference: 400m in descent.
Grade: easy walk, sometimes on gravel paths, sometimes on tarmac.
Refreshments: 2 restaurants in Sete Cidades.

In 1901 the Portuguese king stood on a viewpoint which is still today described as 'of the king'. 'Vista do Rei', clearly the most beautiful viewpoint which the Azores have to offer, is in all the leaflets, picture books and travel guides (see photo on page 32). The view sweeps over Lagoa Verde (green lake), across to Lagoa Azul (blue lake), down to the village of Sete Cidades

and up to the edge of the Lagoa Verde crater as far as Pico da Cruz, 845m, the highest point on the eastern rim of the crater. Red hibiscus flowers here in April and May until it's replaced in summer by blue hydrangeas. The beauty of this landscape attracts many people. There are especially a lot of visitors in July and August at the weekend. The name Sete Cidades (seven towns) goes back to a legend since, in fact, there's only one village in the caldeira, 262m, and not seven towns. It's unusual in the Azores for a village to have established itself in an intact caldeira.

At the starting point of your walk, the **Vista do Rei** viewpoint, the romantic Lagoa Verde (0.75km x 1.4km) glistens in the foreground

The church in Sete Cidades.

and behind it, separated only by a narrow strip of road, Lagoa Azul (2.6km x 2.4km). There's a leisurely path going left from the viewpoint down into the caldeira, past luxuriantly rampant criptomeria (Japenese cedars). After 45 minutes you reach an tarmac road. Turn right onto this. At the point where the tarmac road leads up to **Lagoa Verde** you can make a 45 minute detour by the side of this lagoa and enjoy the wonderful atmosphere. The path ends at a rock face at the southern shore of the lake. Back along the same path you reach the dam. You can continue round the Tufo peninsula and further along **Lagoa Azul** as far as the picnic area where it's possible to have a swim. At the moment you can't walk all the way round the lakes, but shoreline paths are already being planned.

Go back the same way towards **Sete Cidades** which will take you 30 minutes. At the beginning of the village with its white painted houses your attention is caught by the beautiful Residencia Andrade Albuquerque. It belongs to the family of the same name. On the other side of the road there are some wonderful gardens. They are private, but it's worth asking if you can take a look around. If you stay on this road you will come directly to the bus stop. The Lagoa Azul restaurant is opposite. A very beautiful avenue, leading to the church, turns off from this road.

3 From Sete Cidades through the tunnel to Mosteiros

A rather unusual walk

Sete Cidades – Lagoa Azul – tunnel – Mosteiros

Starting point: Sete Cidades, 262m. Bus from Ponta Delgada.
Destination: Mosteiros, 40m. Bus to Ponta Delgada.
Walking time: 1 hour.
Height difference: 220m.
Grade: easy.

Refreshments: restaurants in Mosteiros with fish specialities.
Tips: this walk can be combined with the walk from Vista do Rei to Sete Cidades (Walk 2). Take a torch and waterproof clothing!

Perhaps you have got to know Sete Cidades on the walk down from the Vista do Rei and the fishing village of Mosteiros on the coast walk from Ginetos to Mosteiros and already appreciate this beautiful scenery. Because there is so much to see here and many of the walks are easily combined, here's another suggestion for a walk unlike any other you will find in the Azores.

View from the Vista do Rei of Sete Cidades, Lagoa Verde and Lagoa Azul.

On this walk you will be spared the extremely strenuous climb over the crater rim since this unusual route takes you through the water tunnel towards Mosteiros. This 1385m long tunnel was built in the 1930s so that the lake didn't flood the village after heavy rainstorms. As it is dripping wet in the tunnel you will need waterproof clothing, but it's not dangerous.

Leave the village of **Sete Cidades** on the unsurfaced road towards **Lagoa Azul** (blue lake) and walk beside the lake for a way until you reach the picnic area at the end of the path. Right by the picnic area there's a water channel, called a levada. There's also a bridge to cross over the channel.

On the other side turn left and follow the levada as far as the entrance to the tunnel. It will take 20 minutes to get through and reach daylight again in a wood of Japanese cedars. You have to turn left along the tarmac road. Shortly afterwards you find two hiking paths – one goes up left and the other down right. Choose the right hand one and go downhill. You will soon see the sea and Pico de Mafra, 359m, on the right. Walk to a junction. Turn left here and you soon come to a short path on the right hand side which you follow downhill to **Mosteiros**.

4   From Arribanas to Capelas

Crossing the island by taxi and on foot

Arribanas – Pico do Cedro – Capelas

Starting point: Arribanas, 261m. Take a taxi (no buses).
Destination: Capelas, 10m. Bus to Ponta Delgada.
Walking times: Arribanas – Pico do Cedro 1½ hours, Pico do Cedro – Capelas ½ hour. Total time 2 hours.
Height difference: 251m in descent.
Grade: easy.
Refreshments: restaurant in Capelas.

If you would like to get to know the typical landscape of the 'green' island and at the same time find out the difference between the south coast and the north coast, then this soft touch of a walk is just right. From Ponta Delgada to Arribanas you drive mainly through undulating countryside, past Pico dos Bodes on the right, 310m. On both sides of the road there are the typically white cottages frequently found in the Azores. In Arribanas, 261m, take the gentle and broad path leading northwards with stone walls and hydrangea hedgerows on both sides. The 485m high Pico Serra Gorda is on the right. Then the path goes past a small pond, large boulders and a small quarry. After about 1½ hours you reach a milk collecting place with the inscription 'Lactinos Loreto'.

From Arribanas to Capelas.

CAPELAS

Algueiras
Rosário

Três
Cruzes

Teatro
Novo

Pico do
Cedro
370

ariana
Mulata
373

Monte Alegre

Pico do
Enforcado
341

Charco dos Leimos

Pico do
Negro
307

Pico da Pintona
362

370

Tiçoas

Serra
Gorda
485

Pedra
Queimada

0   1 km

456

Arribanas

The 370m high **Pico do Cedro**, overgrown with thick green shrubs, is on the right hand side. It's part of the Pico area, a plain with many small craters in the north.

You should leave the main path here and take the path to the right which leads gradually downhill. Now you have a marvellous view of the north coast and the picturesque village of Capelas. After descending for 20 minutes you reach a junction and take the path between two houses, now on tarmac again, until you get to the main road in **Capelas** with the STOP sign. Continue right, to the Rossio main square. The bus for Ponta Delgada stops there too.

However, before travelling back, make a detour to the harbour north of Capelas. There's a whale lookout point here, high up on a rock (Vigia de baleia). The harbour bay looks gloomy with its dark rocky wall, quite different from the coastal villages in the south. There are only a few fishing boats still left today.

If you'd rather return by taxi than by bus, go via Fajã de Cima with its picturesque windmills and one of the few churches in the Azores which displays a Gothic style. But the pineapple plantations with their reflecting greenhouses are also interesting. In the shops you can buy anything to do with pineapples.

5 From Lombadas to Ribeira Grande

The wilderness of São Miguel

Lombadas – Ribeira Grande

Starting point: Lombadas, 340m. Travel by taxi (no buses).
Destination: Ribeira Grande, 40m. Bus to Ponta Delgada.
Walking time: 2 hours.

Height difference: 300m in descent.
Grade: relatively easy.
Refreshments: restaurants in Ribeira Grande.

If you only know the landscape of São Miguel with wide green meadows and grazing black and white cows, a peaceful, gentle landscape, then the region here is totally different – wild and craggy, with pointed rock needles which are overgrown with heather and other plants, the furrowed mountain country of Monte Escuro, 890m. This wilderness has a special charm in fog and cloud. Bottles of mineral water were previously filled for the whole island at the Lombadas spring. Many rare plants grow around the former bottling plant and some can only be found on São Miguel.

The hiking path from **Lombadas** to Ribeira Grande is not hard, but it twists all over the place. You just need to keep going straight ahead on the main path. The nearer you get to Ribeira Grande the more the picturesque wilderness fades into the background.

Shortly before the town the path meets the main road which you follow to the left into the centre of **Ribeira Grande**.

With 12,000 inhabitants, Ribeira Grande is the second largest town on the island. The newly built Ponta Delgada link road goes past a geothermic station where electricity is extracted from the volcanic heat of the earth. Ribeira Grande is a beautiful town and the main street in particular has impressive ornate black bars on the windows.

The baroque 'Igreja do Espírito Santo'.

To reach the main square with its three churches go back from the bus stop to the main road and then turn left. The river which cuts the square in two through a deep valley has given its name to the town. A stone bridge connects the two halves of the town. The old men sit in the shade of the trees in front of the baroque church, the donkey carts and mopeds rattle through the archway. The conference hall is worth a visit. A broad flight of steps beyond it leads to the 'Nossa Senhora das Estrelas' church with lots of interesting things to see inside. You should also visit the town museum. The striking baroque church of Igreja do Espírito Santo has a muschelkalk (shelly limestone) façade. You'll find taxis here as well.

6 Over Pico Barrosa, 947m, to Praia

Right across the island to Praia

Sand mine – Pico Barrosa – Lagoa do Fogo – Praia

Starting point: sand mine, 755m, on the road from Ribeira Grande to Lagoa do Fogo. Bus from Ponta Delgada to Ribeira Grande, 20m. From Ribeira Grande by taxi to the sand mine.

Destination: Praia, 57m, suburb of Água de Alto. Bus to Ponta Delgada, Vila Franca do Campo and Povoação.

Walking times: sand mine – Pico Barrosa 1 hour, Pico Barrosa – Lagoa do Fogo ¾ hour, Lagoa do Fogo – Praia 2¼ hours. Total time 4 hours.

Height difference: from the sand mine 200m in ascent and 900m in descent.

Grade: strenuous, requiring good route-finding ability. Descent to Lagoa do Fogo possibly muddy and slippery.

Refreshments: restaurant-café in Praia.

Tip: if you would like to walk across the whole island, in Ribeira Grande go from the last bus stop for the buses from Ponta Delgada to the main street, continue right and go left at the church into the narrow Rua de S. Sebastião (sign 'Lagoa do Fogo'). There's a grocer's shop in front of the church where you can buy supplies – nothing can be bought during the rest of the walk.

The alleyway, lined with one storey houses, goes gently uphill. As you head out of the village on an tarmac road there are meadows on the left and the right with black and white cows. There's no shade so take a hat and sun-cream with you. Quite a lot of lorries travel along this road and the scenery is not particularly interesting.

After 2 hours when you have reached the sand mine at 730m, continue as described below.

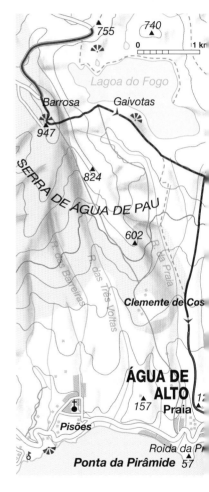

Hot springs near Lagoa do Fogo.

For this strenuous and difficult walk you should read the description and look at the map carefully due to the route-finding problems. Wait for settled weather and do not walk on your own!

Coming from Ribeira Grande by taxi get out at the **sand mine** at the fork in the path, take the path on the right, walk 15 paces along this to the right around the sand mine towards a small wood. You come to a junction. Stay at the edge of the wood on the right hand side and continue uphill. At the next fork go back onto the track and uphill round several bends. Still going uphill you reach **Pico Barrosa**, 947m.

From Pico go down a little way left to a grassy path along a ridge which stretches from the rim of the Lagoa do Fogo crater down to the sea. This path ends at the remains of some buildings and channels. Through these ruins you come to a track which continues over the mountain ridge. Keep to the side of the wood and look for a place to make a suitable descent cross-country to **Lagoa do Fogo**. Be careful – the descent to Lagoa do Fogo can be muddy and slippery if there are damp mists rising. At Lagoa do Fogo go right to the Gaivotas viewpoint and then, as in Walk 7, continue to **Praia**, a suburb of Água de Alto.

7   From Praia to Lagoa do Fogo and back

Dark and rather eerie

Praia – Lagoa do Fogo – Gaivotas – Praia

Starting point and destination: 'O'Aranjo' café in Praia, 57m, a suburb of Água de Alto. Bus from Ponta Delgada, Vila Franca do Campo or Povoação. The central bus stop in Praia is next to the café.
Walking times: Praia – Lagoa do Fogo 3 hours, Lagoa do Fogo – Gaivotas ½ hour, Gaivotas – Praia 2½ hours. Total time 6 hours.
Height difference: 600m in ascent and descent.
Grade: easy, but be careful on the descent to the lake.
Refreshments: restaurant-café in Praia.

The enormous caldeira originated in 1653 after a volcanic eruption and Lagoa do Fogo (fire lake) later resulted from this. The lake, 600m, is the highest in São Miguel and the breeding territory for hundreds of seagulls (Gaivotas). You should choose a fine day for this walk as the dark Lagoa do Fogo can quickly become enveloped in thick mist so that, without a compass, it's difficult to find your bearings. Apart from sturdy hiking boots, you should take some food, drinking water and rain gear, as nothing can be bought on the way.

The walk begins at the 'O'Aranjo' café in **Praia**. Cross over the road and go a short way in the direction of Vila Franca do Campo. At the turn-off ascend left up an unsurfaced path through a countryside of meadows and fields. Then follows a wooded area with large trees.

Eventually the path goes through low tree heathers, in places along a channel, and then later through grasses and ferns. (There are no snakes in the Azores so you don't need to worry when walking through the ferns). The path always keeps to the left hand side of the Ribeira da Praia. It leads across a dense mossy plateau down to **Lagoa do Fogo**.

Lagoa do Fogo crater lake with a diameter of 6km is a nature reserve with many endemic plants. On its north side there are sand and volcanic ash beaches. The whole crater generally has a very sombre atmosphere even when a ray of sun breaks through the clouds now and then.

The descent down to the water is not dangerous, but you need to be careful not to slip. Below at the lake you will find pumice stones and you can listen to them clicking together in the water. There's also a small meteorological station here. Many Azoreans believe that this rather eerie lake is haunted.

You can now return on the same path back to Praia. However it makes a change to continue walking to the right, past the **Gaivotas** viewpoint. This path leads down on the other side of the Ribeira da Praia, past a shepherds' shelter cut into the rock.

After you have left behind the area of low tree heathers (Erica azorica) and gone past some tall trees, you pass a farmstead on the left hand side.

Continue right at a cattle trough, through an area of fields and vegetables until you reach the first houses and come back to the bus stop in **Praia** again.

Lagoa do Fogo has a rather sombre atmosphere.

8 From Vila Franca do Campo to the 'Nossa Senhora da Paz' chapel

A really special destination for a walk

Vila Franca do Campo – 'Nossa Senhora da Paz' chapel and back

Starting point and destination: Vila Franca do Campo church, 20m. Bus from Ponta Delgada.
Walking time: 1¼ hours.

Height difference: 200m in ascent and descent.
Grade: easy.
Refreshments: Vila Franca do Campo.

This unusual destination for a walk, the 'Nossa Senhora da Paz' chapel, is a possibility for days when, for example, the clouds are gathering in the mountains and you can pack your swimming things and walk along the coast. Vila Franca do Campo, today with about 7,000 inhabitants, was once the capital of the island. In 1522 it was destroyed by an earthquake. Rich people moved to Ponta Delgada which was declared the capital in 1546. What's striking about Vila Franca do Campo is the chequered lay-out of the streets. 'São Miguel' church is one of the few 'black' churches remaining in the Azores from that great time and built out of dark basalt stone. The remains of a protection wall near the fishing harbour are evidence of former pirate attacks. It gets lively in the harbour around midday, when the fishermen return with their catch. The Ilhéu da Vila Franca rises up out of the sea in front of Vila Franca do Campo. It is of volcanic origin and since June, a much sought-after bathing spot. You can swim in the shelter of the rocks as if in a private swimming pool and you can get a boat here from the harbour. The whole island is a nature reserve.

'Nossa Senhora da Paz' pilgrims' chapel.

The destination for this short walk is the 'Nossa Senhora da Paz' pilgrims' chapel situated to the north on a hill. It is unique in the Azores and you are unlikely to find a pilgrims' chapel towering up so impressively out of the landscape in other catholic countries.

Start the walk on the road which leads uphill next to the church in **Vila Franca do Campo**. Here you'll find a sign for the pilgrims' chapel. The path goes past some houses at first, then along the Ribeira da Mãa de Agua, past vegetable gardens, orange plantations and meadows. The view of the chapel is striking.

After half an hour the road turns away from the river. Two bends follow which lead steeply uphill until you reach the start of the steps up to the **'Nossa Senhora da Paz' chapel**. The steps have ten landings which you can climb onto from the right or the left. On each landing there's a wall with blue and white tiles, the so-called azulejos, which depict a scene from the Holy Scriptures. It's often claimed that the azulejos come from the Flemish who were driven from their homeland for religious reasons and came to settle in the Azores. But that's not the case. The azulejos took a quite different path. The Moors brought them to Spain, from where they came over to Portugal and then it wasn't far to the Azores.

Once at the top by the chapel you have a marvellous view of Vila Franca do Campo, the Ilhéu da Vila Franca and the sea. At the back of the chapel there's a shrine to the Virgin Mary which is highly revered.

Return along the same path.

9 Around Lagoa das Furnas

Where the earth steams and bubbles

Furnas – Lagoa das Furnas – campsite – Furnas

Starting point and destination: Furnas, 245m. Bus Ponta Delgada and Povoação.
Walking times: Furnas – Lagoa ½ hour, round path as far as the camp site 3 hours, campsite – Furnas ¾ hour. Total time 4¼ hours.
Height difference: 80m ascent and descent.
Grade: easy.
Refreshments: restaurants in Furnas.

The area around Furnas is a paradise of park and flowers, but also a region where the earth doesn't come to rest. Furnas itself lies in a large, collapsed caldera with a diameter of 6km and it is surrounded by high, wooded rock faces. The volcanic part of the Azores islands is to be found here with bubbling mud pots, hot springs, sulphur pools and small geysers – also to be found in and around Furnas lake.

The walk begins in **Furnas** at the church. Follow the main street in the direction of Vila Franca do Campo, past the 'Terra Nostra' hotel, and before the end of the village turn onto a narrow tarmac road which ascends up between small houses and a stream. Where the houses finish it becomes a path which goes along the edge of a wood. On the right is the Ribeira do

The sulphur pools at Furnas.

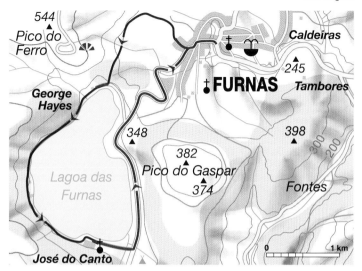

Fogo valley. At two houses the path bends sharply to the left and goes leisurely up and down at the foot of the crater rim south-westwards. Then the
path turns sharply to the left again and goes downhill. Continue along a
broad grassy path, shortly afterwards going up steeply to a mountain ridge
and then down again steeply. Now you see **Lagoa das Furnas**.

You are met by a smell of sulphur. There's a small picnic area on a hill with a
wonderful panorama. Continuing right you come to the mud pots
(fumaroles). Many local families use these for cooking at the weekends.
Meat and vegetables are sunk into the mud in tightly sealed pots and after
three to four hours the food is cooked (cozido). There's another picnic area
further on, then you come to the edge of the wood, walk on a gravel path
along the wooded shoreline and go past a thick grove of bamboo. You see
old villas, surrounded by araucarias, dragon trees and other exotic plants.
The gravel road goes past the José do Canto chapel which a Portuguese
couple had built by a Parisian architect as a graveyard chapel.

Then you come to a **campsite** and meet the main road which you follow to
the left as far as **Furnas**.

There's a bus stop in Largo da Praia e Montfort square near the entrance to
the Terra Nostra park. The bus going north, and therefore the shorter connection to Ponta Delgada, leaves from this bus stop while the bus along the
south coast to Ponta Delgada and the bus to Provoaçao leave from outside
the general store.

10 From Furnas to Lagoa Secca and Pico do Gaspar

São Miguel's paradise of flowers

Furnas – Lagoa Secca – Pico do Gaspar – Furnas

Starting point and destination: Terra Nostra park in Furnas, 245m. Bus from Ponta Delgada and Povoação.
Walking times: Terra Nostra park in Furnas – Lagoa Secca 1¼ hours, Lagoa Secca – Pico do Gaspar – Furnas 1 hour. Total time 2¼ hours.
Height difference: 150m in ascent and descent.
Grade: rather slippery in places.
Refreshments: restaurants in Furnas.

The surrounding area of Furnas is something special – you could even say unique – and not because of its volcanic appearance such as hot springs and geysers. So it's worth doing more than one walk there. Furnas is the oldest tourist town on São Miguel and its valley a sea of flowers, shining red in spring with azalea and rhododendron blossom and replaced by blue hydrangeas in June.

Altogether 22 different mineral waters are to be found bubbling at the Centro Termal de Furnas (health spa) with varying temperatures and constitu-

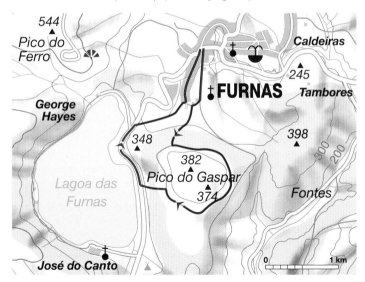

The Terra Nostra park with hotel and thermal pool.

ents. The 'Caldeira Grande', for example, supplies 99 °C hot water, 61 litres a minute. The waters are supposed to help rheumatism and skin diseases. Of course, the locals know which is the best one for every affliction from amongst the 22 varieties.

It was in the 17th century when they began to discover the healing power of mineral waters. The nobles and business people of Ponta Delgada chose Furnas for their summer residence. The first was Thomas Hicking in 1770, the American Vice Consul who laid the foundation for the Terra Nostra park by having tropical plants planted there. During subsequent centuries well-to-do families imported rare exotic plants to brighten up their grounds. Terra Nostra park, which is now 20 hectares and borders directly on the Terra Nostra hotel, is the most beautiful park in the Azores, and is criss-crossed by many attractive footpaths. A warm, iron-bearing stream and a cold, clear one flow through the park, ideal for particular plants like araucarias, bamboo, cedars, water lilies, magnolia, camelias, hibiscus, jacaranda, giant ferns and others. Here you can also take a cure and bathe in a large pool at a temperature of 40 °C. Don't forget to take your swimming thing with you!

The walk begins and ends in **Furnas** at the main gateway of the Terra Nostra park. When you leave the park turn to the left and walk beside the park railings as far as the crossroads, then continue straight on, ascending and

47

São Miguel

Lagoa das Furnas.

descending along an tarmac link road. On the left there's a cemetery with a chapel. Then it goes steeper uphill through wooded countryside. Looking back you have a lovely view of the white houses in Furnas, the meadows and the gardens.

Continue a short way uphill, then coming out of the wood you have a view of **Lagoa Secca** (dry lake), 374m, and **Pico do Gaspar**, 382m, a truly strange landscape. The sea is in the south. Follow the narrow path on the left hand side which gently ascends up to the ridge.

You have many beautiful views of the sea where the Japanese cedars (Cryptomeria japonica), reaching sometimes as high as 20m, do not obscure the view. They were introduced in Europe in 1844 and grow very fast and supply good fuel – ideal for exporting. 70 percent of the Azorean cedars grow on São Miguel. The original laurel wood and the other plants as well don't stand a chance against the cedar. This trend towards a mono-culture is continually altering the shape of the landscape.

After a quarter of an hour from the ridge you can see the glistening Furnas lake. In late summer the path can be overgrown with ginger plants, but otherwise there are no problems. Keeping Lagoa Secca always on your right hand side you come into a pine forest after another 15 minutes. Then the path meets the tarmac road which you follow to the right along the lake for a while.

Now you can descend a narrow path through the wood on the right hand side. The path goes past a white farm house. After half an hour there's a fork. Take the right hand path through the cedars.

Before the path continues to descend you can make another detour to a garden with high hedges. It is run by the government and countless azaleas and camelias are planted there to be used as cut flowers. If the gate is open you can take a look at the garden.

After you have left the cedars behind, the path goes fairly steeply down to **Furnas** in 15 minutes.

The sulphur pools at Furnas.

Santa Maria, the good weather island

The Columbus memorial in Anjos.

Santa Maria, the eastern island of the Azores, is geologically unique compared to its brothers and sisters – it is supposed to have risen out of the sea 160 million years ago, in the Jurassic period. There are no mud pots, there's no caldeira, no volcanic eruptions, no earthquakes. 17km long and 9.5km wide, it is one of the small ones. Flat in the west, mountainous in the east, and the highest mountain, Pico Alto, is only 587m high, nevertheless an ideal viewpoint over to São Miguel. Santa Maria is ideal for island lovers: people who love white beaches, spend their day at leisure, walk and don't expect anything to happen. You fly to the island on a small SATA plane. There's a ferry connection planned with São Miguel, but that would also encourage more tourists.

Diogo de Silves is said to have discovered the island in 1427 on the saint's day of the Virgin which gave it the name of Santa Maria. In 1439 the Portuguese Gonçalo Velho Cabral came to take up post as captain of the island with a ship which was loaded with settlers and seeds. The settlers came from the Algarve coast which you can still see today in the construction of the houses. They founded Santana, Anjos, Praia and, as a harbour, Vila. In 1493 on his return from the Caribbean islands Columbus anchored offshore from Anjos to pray and to stock up with provisions. There are various stories about his arrival. At first they thought he was a pirate, until his identity could be proved after a lot of toing and froing. He prayed in the old church of Anjos of which today only the archway remains, and in the year of Columbus, 1993, the islanders erected a memorial in his honour. For centuries the settlers had problems with pirates, evidence of which is the fort outside Vila do Porto armed with canons. The attacks by pirates resulted in more and more settlers emigrating to Brazil.

People lived from the cultivation of woad, which produces a blue dye, and a lichen (orchil) which gives a very good brown dye. Up to the 17th century the blue colours were sold to Flanders, England and Spain but they were displaced by the indigo from Brazil. Brown remained in demand until chemical dyes came onto the market in the 19th century. The settlers worked for about 16 big landowners until the island was divided up in 1590 and each family received a piece of land. Today there are 6000 inhabitants of which 2800 live in Vila do Porto.

During the second World War circumstances changed when the Allies received authorisation for the building of two airport bases. A 3km long runway was built on Santa Maria for trans-Atlantic flight changeovers which is no longer necessary today. But the airport is still the largest income provider of the island with 500 employees who have made their homes around the airport. At present it's chiefly the Holy Spirit charter planes which land here at the time of the festival, from Boston and Toronto with Azorean emigrants who have remained in contact with their homeland. Many of those who returned to Santa Maria have built themselves a little house with a garden for growing vegetables and keeping pigs and have retired there. The agricultural Santa Maria has a lot going for it – reliable weather, the shops in Vila do Porto's main street where you can buy everything you need, and the short distance from São Miguel and Ponta Delgada for times when bigger shopping expeditions need to be made, you have to go on important business or you simply want to take part in the festivities in Ponta Delgada.

Typical farmhouse on Santa Maria.

Santa Maria

Two hotels, one at the airport and one in Vila do Porto, offer accommodation, as well as Apartementos Turisticos at the Praia Formosa near Vila do Porto, with favourable prices and recommended if you are wanting to stay a little longer on Santa Maria. The tourist office managed only by a single person (Posto de Turismo) is situated in the airport. The beautiful white beaches on this island of good weather are inviting places to sunbathe, but the intensity of the sun's rays make the use of effective sun-cream absolutely imperative.

A SUMMARY OF INFORMATION ABOUT SANTA MARIA

Formigas, caves and fossils

The small islands near Santa Maria are called Formigas or Ilhéus. Eight ilhéus are under environmental protection as nesting places for sea birds. You can visit the island of Romeiro. It's situated at the end of São Lourenço bay and has a cave with stalagmites and stalactites. For cave lovers there are the caves of Santana, Baia do Cura, Cré, Agua, Velho and Faneca, but only with experienced companions and the necessary equipment. 'Ossos de Gigantes' (giant bones) are what the locals call the ancient fossils of molluscs and other sea animals from the Tertiary Period found on the oldest Azorean island.

Best time to travel

As it hardly ever rains on Santa Maria, May is the best time to travel and hike, for then you will see the island in brilliant green and the flowers in bloom. Later in the year it gets dry and the ground turns yellow, especially in the flat south-west.

Transport

Public transport is a bit thin on the ground. Buses take the children to school and back. You can get a timetable from the posto turismo. If you want a short introduction to the island take a round trip by taxi. If you're walking, take a taxi to the starting point and order it for your return from the other end. For some time now on Santa Maria you have been able to hire a car.

Island festivals

The festivals of the Holy Spirit (Festas do Espírito Santo) which the settlers from Portugal brought with them and which you will also come across on other islands, are celebrated with processions on Santa Maria. There are also decorated ox-drawn carts which bring 'food to the needy', women with bread and wine and ornate metal crowns. The Vila do Porto Festival on the 15th August is the most important one on Santa Maria and one of the most significant in the archipelago.
The festivals of the individual island patron saints also take place in summer. The question 'where?' is easy to answer – 'where the noise is coming from.' A modern event is the Maré de Agosto music festival at the end of August, with jazz, rock and folk music.

Sights

The churches of Vila do Porto, Almagreira and Santa Bárbara are always worth a visit. You will see immediately that they do not have the same glittery gold richness of the São Miguel churches.

On the way to Praia.

11 From Santa Bárbara onto Pico Alto

Onto the highest mountain on the island

Santa Bárbara – Cruz dos Picos – Pico Alto and back

Starting point and destination: Church in Santa Bárbara, 287m. Bus from Vila do Porto at 7 and at 13.30. Return from Santa Bárbara by taxi.
Walking times: Santa Bárbara – Pico Alto 1½ hours, return 1 hour. Total time 2½ hours.
Height difference: 300m in ascent and descent.
Grade: easy, except for last part on the summit which is steep and rather strenuous. Danger of slipping on loose stones.
Refreshments: restaurant in Santa Bárbara, not always open.
Tip: talk with the taxi driver on the way there about when to be picked up at the other end. You must expect to be charged for the waiting time as the driver is usually unable to make any other trips in the meantime.

If you want to do several walks on Santa Maria this is a good one to begin with since there's an excellent view over the island from the summit.

The walk begins at the simple, but impressive church in **Santa Bárbara** (well worth a visit!). Take the main path to the left and go straight on past a cattle trough and afterwards an old well. Then there's a fork. Take the left hand path which ascends quite steeply uphill after you have left the last houses behind you. When you reach the junction continue left. This path is not so steep and goes across a hillside until after a few minutes it meets an tarmac road. Continue to the right to a fork in the road, '**Cruz dos Picos**'. Keep right here. After about 30m you turn off right again onto the path to Pico Alto which leads uphill through a wood on small bends.

After about 20 minutes you reach a conspicuous gap in the rocks. A small concrete house has been built into the hillside on the left and from in front some rather steep steps lead up to the summit of Pico Alto, 587m. Here you have a wonderful panorama, spoilt only a little by the telecommunication sites. What's interesting is the contrast between the fairly densely populated flat western half of the island and the hilly, green and thinly populated eastern half where Santa Bárbara lies, the largest town.

In the north-west you see a red, desert-like region which you will become acquainted with in Walk 15. In clear visibility you can just see the island of São Miguel, 90km in the distance.

Return along the same path.

View from Pico Alto.

12 Stroll to São Lourenço

The most beautiful sandy bay in the Azores

Santa Barbara – Arrebentão – Miradouro – São Lourenço and back

Starting point and destination: Santa Bárbara, 287m. Bus from Vila do Porto at 7.00 and at 13.30.
Walking times: Santa Bárbara – São Lourenço ¾ hour, detour to the Miradouro ½ hour, return 1 hour. Total time 2¼ hours.
Height difference: just under 300m in ascent and descent.
Grade: very easy.
Refreshments: restaurant in Santa Bárbara, not always open.
Tip: as you can't expect eating places in Santa Bárbara to be open, always take some food with you. No shopping opportunities in São Lourenço.

Lovers of the archipelago are united on one thing – São Lourenço is the most beautiful sandy bay in the Azores – even if as to opinions the most beautiful island differ quite a lot. If you decide to go on this walk from Santa Bárbara to São Lourenço, you must take into account the slight disadvantage of the path to the bay and back going along a narrow tarmac side road. You can lessen the effect on your knees and the small of your back with cushion-soled walking shoes and walking poles. Don't forget to take swimming things with you on sunny days.

Santa Bárbara, together with Santo Espírito, Almagreia and São Pedro, is one of the most beautiful places on the island. Emigrants from the Algarve coast settled in Santa Bárbara as well as other places and they brought their architecture with them: shining white buildings with blue window frames. You also occasionally see red painted frames and railings – to ward off evil spirits, supposedly. Characteristic are the large round fire places.

View of São Lourenço.

From **Santa Bárbara** go along the main road to **Arrebentão** (both places merge into one) and from there gently downhill along a narrow side road in the direction of the coast. The small road goes through soft green valleys and after half an hour goes downhill round three rather steep bends. Keep to the right after the last bend and go inland round a wide curve until you reach a **miradouro**, a very beautiful viewpoint which is surrounded by flowering azaleas, arum lilies or hydrangeas, depending on the time of year. From here you have a broad view of the Baia do São Lourenço and just in the foreground, Ilhéu de São Lourenço – a place to sit for a while.

After a short break return along the last section to the road and you will come to the 1 km long **São Lourenço** bay with a sandy beach, and then the little road with the holiday homes behind. Steepening slopes stretch above where wine is cultivated.

The vines, planted in the Azorean way (see Walk 13), are enclosed with dark stone walls to lessen the danger of landslides, and at the same time there's no wind in the bay.

If you rent a room with a sea view for the night you will make two very striking observations – the glimmering lights of Formigas after dark and an indescribably beautiful sunrise the next morning.

13 From Fonte do Jórdão via Panasco, Piedade and Malbusca to Praia

Through the vineyards on the south coast

Fonte do Jórdão – Panasco – Malbusca – Alem – Barreiros – Praia

Starting point: Fonte do Jórdão, 270m. Take a taxi (there are no buses).
Destination: Praia, 10m. Return to Fonte do Jórdão by taxi.
Walking times: Fonte do Jórdão – Panasco ¾ hour, Panasco – Malbusca ½ hour, Malbusca – Praia 2½ hours. Total time 3¾ hours.
Height difference: 260m in descent.
Grade: easy.

Refreshments: in the high season restaurant in Praia.
Tip: you can do this walk in reverse in conjunction with Walk 14 (from Vila do Porto to Praia), then it's a considerable 5 to 6 hours of continuous walking time. However it's recommended that you walk in the direction described here so that you can enjoy the view through the vineyards.

This walk is one of the most beautiful on Santa Maria as the view sweeps through the vineyards and on the other side across the blue sea glistening with white crested waves.

In **Fonte do Jórdão** go a few steps southwards through the small village with the shining white houses as far as a narrow path which leaves the village downhill to the left, at first through a small wood then into the vineyards. There is in fact a gravel road which turns off left north of Fonte do Jórdão and goes downhill via Malbusca to Praia, but it is not as attractive as this narrow path which goes through the vineyards and up along the coast giving a wonderful view of the sea and Baia da Praia.

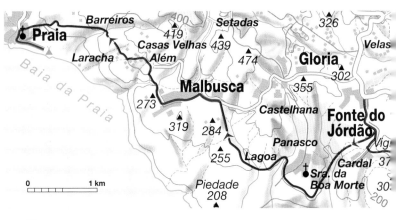

Through the vineyards to Praia.

The vineyards are built on terraces and separated with dark stone walls so that they each form a square or a rectangle. 6 to 15 vines are planted in each one depending on the size. The southern slopes and the warmth of the retaining stone walls ensure good quality vines. From the southern end of Fonte do Jórdão there's a detour on a small path through the vineyards up to the 373m high Vigia hill from where there's a fantastic view of Ponta (isthmus) do Castelo lighthouse.

Back at the end of Fonte do Jórdão village the path goes first at a height of 270m through a little wood of bushes, then it bends to the right and goes leisurely downhill towards the south to reach the hamlet of **Panasco**, 15 houses and a church, shining white amongst the green of the vineyards. You've now reached a height of 200m. Cross over two placid streams and follow the path gently going uphill to **Malbusca** with about 40 scattered houses and a small road. At the end of the road take the path across the vine terraces again, instead of continuing along the gravel road which, incidentally, is to be surfaced in tarmac. The next hamlet you reach is **Alem**. Walk from here at the same height to **Barreiros** and then descend round two bends to **Praia**.

14 From Vila do Porto to Praia

To the beach that is popular for swimming on the south coast

Vila do Porto – Touril – Brasil – Praia and back

Starting point and destination: Vila do Porto, 20m. Take a taxi (no buses).
Walking times: Vila do Porto – Touril ½ hour, Touril – Praia 1 hour, return 1½ hours. Total time 3 hours.
Height difference: 378m in ascent and descent.
Grade: easy.
Refreshments: restaurant in Praia in the high season. It's a good idea to take some food with you as restaurants etc. might be closed.

At the end of the main street of **Vila do Porto** walk past the houses under a preservation order but not yet restored, over the pavements with the beautiful white mosaics to Fort São Bras high above the harbour. From the battlements with the very rusty canons there's a good view of the harbour and eastwards to Praia bay. At the entrance to the fort there's a small house with an exhibition of paintings and inside the 'Nossa Senhora da Conceição' chapel. The fort is to be restored and its excellent location to be put to better use (as a museum).

From the fort walk up the main street with the 'Nossa Senhora da Vitoria' parish church on the right, dating from the 17th century and rebuilt many times. Turn off right from the main street behind the church. After about 50m the path turns to the left and you are looking down onto the little river, Ribeira de São Francisco. Descend through a meadow, full of campanula in spring, and on stepping stones, cross the little river which rarely has a lot of water.

On the other bank you come to an old trading path which leads eastwards across the hillside. From this path there's a beautiful view back to Vila do Porto and the fort. Wind turbines, originally from Germany, appear ahead. They are due to increase in number since they have been very successful.

The path gets wider and leaving Figueiral, 162m, on the right hand side, you gradually ascend 100m across flat pasture-land which is divided by low walls and can be yellow, depending on the time of year. You see water troughs for livestock, mainly sheep. You will notice the solitary lava boulders in the pastures which the cows use to rub themselves against.

Ascend up to 165m and then continue at the same height, with Facho hill, 254m, on the right hand side, until you come to the small hamlet of **Touril**. On the maps it is sometimes indicated as south, sometimes as more to the east.

From there go along a largely overgrown path northwards to the hamlet of Brasil. This path goes between **Brasil** and Carreira onto another path going south-east onto which you turn down right. It is covered in blackberry brambles in places and can be quite slippery. Then you come to a road which leads from Almagreira via the hamlet of Brejo to Praia and you walk on tarmac round some bends to **Praia**. This path goes past some solitary shining white farm houses and holiday bungalows. The exceptionally beautiful Praia bay is very popular, an ideal beach for swimming. It consists of limy sea sediment which is several millions of years old. If you lie down you will notice that it's not especially warm, as the sediment doesn't retain the heat as well as normal sand.

After a lengthy stop for a swim **return** to Vila do Porto on the same path.

Lighthouse above Praia bay.

15 To the 'Nossa Senhora da Fátima' chapel

Through the aluminium oxide wastes of Deserto de Faneco

Columbus memorial in Anjos – 'Nossa Senhora do Pilar' chapel – Deserto de Faneco – 'Nossa Senhora da Fátima' chapel

Starting point: Columbus memorial in Anjos, 10m. Take a taxi.
Destination: 'Nossa Senhora da Fátima' chapel, 220m. Return by taxi (no buses).

Walking time: 2 hours.
Height difference: 200m.
Grade: easy, partly on tarmac road.
Refreshments: none.

There has been some talk about Anjos, the oldest village on the island, in conjunction with the landing of Columbus. When you reach the village your gaze falls immediately on the modern Columbus memorial of 1993. This is where the walk begins. There's only a basalt gateway remaining from the oldest church on Santa Maria, if not on all the islands in the Azores, in which Columbus is supposed to have offered up a prayer of thanks with his crew on their return from the Caribbean islands. Right by the side there's a new church which is simple, but again has striking azure-blue paint and a triptych which Gonçalo Velho, the discoverer of Santa Maria, is said to have brought with him.

On the way from Anjos to the 'Nossa Senhora da Fátima' chapel.

Diagonally behind the **Columbus memorial** there are some gleaming white houses, behind them a wooden fence with a small gate. It would be more polite to ask first if you can go through. You are allowed to, of course, but a little bit of politeness in the Azores goes a long way. Behind the fence go uphill across a meadow, with the little Ribeira do Lemos river on your right, climb easily over three stone walls and reach a path leading north-east. You pass by an old farmstead where banana plants are cultivated. The path continues uphill and you reach the hilly part of the island with Monte Gordo, 184m, on the left and Monte Flores, 297m, on the right. The path gets sandier. Past the **'Nossa Senhora do Pilar' chapel** you approach the aluminium oxide wastes of **Deserto de Faneco**. The sight of this desert is fairly unexpected – a plain of red sand with hardly a single plant, secluded, and sometimes a motorbike rider at the most roaring through the sand. Aluminium oxide was once mined here for Santa Maria pottery.

After a 50 minute crossing of the Deserto de Faneco you come to a trading path. Past some farms the path meets a narrow tarmac road onto which you turn left. The region now returns to its agricultural character. The path along the tarmac takes about 1 hour, but the destination is worth it. Turn left when you reach the main road.

After about 2km you come to the **'Nossa Senhora da Fátima' chapel** on a steep hill on the left hand side of the road. There are as many steps as there are rosary beads and they are divided into sets in accordance with the chapters of the rosary.

At the top you have a magnificent panorama of the northern part of the island which is more arid and deserted than the southern part. A big festival is celebrated in and around the chapel on the 13th May, the day of the apparition of the Virgin Mary in Fátima.

Terceira, the island of contrasts

The first waymarkings, put up by the 'Os Montanheiros' hiking club.

Terceira is, after São Miguel and Pico, the third largest island in the Azores. The number of inhabitants is half as many as on São Miguel. Over an area of 30km long and 17km wide this island of contrasts has much to offer. More than 30 villages have been established in the coastal area, organised into Creeados (areas separated by dry stone walls). Terceira is divided into a gentle range of mountains, Serra do Cume, in the east, the crater of Caldeira de Guilherme Moniz (the largest of the archipelago with a circumference of 15km) and small craters and lakes in the centre and a volcanic peak with a large crater lake, Serra de Santa Bárbara, in the west.

In the course of history Terceira has been occupied alternately between Spain and Portugal. In the 15th and the 16th centuries the harbour was a trans-shipment centre for gold, silver, diamonds and spices and as a result, an attraction for pirates. It's worth taking the time to read more about the history of Terceira than is given here.

In the 1940s an international airport with three runways was built in Lajes, 3km from Praia da Vitória. It is used for both civilian and military traffic.

Planes from Europe and the USA land here and if you want to reach one of the other islands you will have to make a stopover in Terceira. A unit of the American airforce also has its base here. That's why it's sometimes said that Terceira is americanised, but that's not really true because the island is as Azorean as its eight sisters – only around the airport has there been too much new development.

In the lava regions of Picos da Bagacina es do Carito in the middle of the island, bulls are reared for the 'Tourada a Corda', a bloodless bullfight whereby the bull is tied to a long rope in the street and anyone can approach to prove how brave they are – even with a walking stick or an umbrella. The bullfights take place in every village in the summer and are very popular. They are supposed to have originated in the 16th century in the battle of Salga when an Augustinian monk, Frei Pedro, had the idea of letting 1000 cattle loose on the Spaniards who were attacking them and who subsequently withdrew.

On Terceira the impérios play an especially big role – small, colourfully painted chapels which are said to originate from an initiative by Queen Isabella of Aragon, the wife of King Dinis. The Espírito Santo Festivals (Festivals of the Holy Spirit) are ceremonies in honour of the Holy Spirit and used to serve as a means for bringing to the needy. If the village is celebrating a festival today, everyone is invited to the Sopa do Espírito Santo (soup of the Holy Spirit). The food is served at a table in front of the altar.

A SUMMARY OF INFORMATION ABOUT TERCEIRA

Transport

There are buses between Angra do Heroísmo and Praia da Vitória as well as between Angra do Heroísmo and Biscoitos. Buses travel also between Biscoitos and Praia as well as Lajes and Praia. As the bus services concentrate on the coast you will need a taxi in some circumstances to reach the starting point of your walk.

Grottoes and caves

Algar do Carvão is a geological nature reserve with two grottoes, about 100m deep, a lake and very beautiful stalactites and stalagmites in the interior. A paradise for cave lovers. There are also the grottoes of Balcões, Agulhas and Natal and the caves of Agua and Cabrito. The grottoes and caves originated when gases escaped in the lava as it cooled. You will need a guide to visit the cave and the necessary equipment.

'Os Montanheiros'

'Os Montanheiros' is a club of mountain walkers who go hiking on Terceira and other islands and have a particular interest in the Algar do Carvão cave (Angra do Heroísmo, Rua da Rocha, 6–8, tel. 2 29 92); telephone them if you can speak some Portuguese.

Sights

Wine museum in Biscoitos.

Angra do Heroísmo

The capital of Terceira is certainly an interesting place to visit and was included by UNESCO in 1983 on its World Heritage list. The town received its epithet of 'do Heroísmo' in the 19th century for the achievements of its citizens in the various wars.

Angra (harbour in a bay) was designed on the drawing board and protection against the winds was included into the plans. During the course of centuries houses might have changed their façades, but the town retains its original outline. It quickly became an important and rich trade centre and seat of the bishopric. Splendid palaces and churches were built in the time of the Renaissance. Pirates in the 17th to 19th centuries repeatedly tried to plunder Angra. The 'Castelo de São Filipe' castle dates from this time and later became known as 'São João Baptista'.

On January 1st 1980 Angra was badly destroyed by an earthquake – 7.8 on the Richter scale. The reconstruction of the architectural monuments is today almost finished. Due to the protection of historic monuments all houses had to be restored in their original form, with the exception of the imperios.

The cathedral on Rua da Sé from the 15th century is the largest church and the only cathedral in the Azores. It is dedicated to São Salvador and was carefully restored. Particularly impressive are the high altar, the cedar wood ceiling, tiles, pictures, ornate silver work, Brazilian rosewood furniture and paintings of the bishops.

Behind the cathedral on the way to the harbour stands Bettencourt palace, a baroque building from the 17th century, built by the rich Azorean Bettencourt family. The rooms with cedar wood panelling today house the public library and the archive of Angra do Heroísmo. The contents date back to the 16th century (400,000 published works and two million documents). The azulejos in the entrance hall are quite beautiful.

Another few steps and you reach the 'Baia de Angra' harbour. You will see the 'Misericórdia' church from the 18th century with interesting paintings and sculptures, built on the spot where the first Azorean hospital was erected in 1492.

Go past the Igreja da Misericórdia and you reach the narrow streets of the historical part of the town and the busy market on Rua do Rego where fruit, vegetables, fish and meat are for sale. Behind the market you come to Rua do João Corte Real and then Largo do Prior do Crato. The former Jesuit convent is to be found on Rua do Marquês. In the middle of the 18th century it was the official residence of the Captain General and today is marked on the town map as the palace of the governor. The Colégio dos Jesuitas is situated behind with many azulejos and gilded carvings. Then you come to Praça da Restauração, also called Praça Velha, the most popular place in town. You'll find the taxis and the bus stops there, also the town hall and Angra hotel. It's not far from here to the municipal park (Jardim Publico) and

Angra do Heroísmo.

beyond that, the Convento de São Francisco with the red and white façade, where Angra museum is housed. Here you can see ceramics, porcelain, paintings, musical instruments, weapons and folk art. If you stroll west-wards down Rua da Sé, the main street, you can marvel at the beautiful façades of the houses with their wrought-iron balconies and window bars. The Esperança monastery, founded in the second half of the 16th century, is on the right hand side. Angra was and is a devout town with nine monas-teries altogether. Continue down the street and the Igreja São Gonçalo rises up, the oldest church in the town, joined to the monastery of Clarissinen. In the church you will find marvellous gilded carvings, azulejos, sculptures and paintings. Next door is to be found the Boa Nova Hospital, supposedly the first military hospital in the world.

It would take too long to describe all the interesting buildings here – in the turismo next to the cathedral you will get some friendly advice and a town plan, a bus time-table, a map of the island on which all the restaurants are marked, and a plan of the Algar do Carvão caves. A special tip is the 'Quinta da Nasce-Água' hotel, 3km from town, very tastefully furnished, with a swimming pool and a very attractive park with tropical plants and trees.

16 Stroll up to Monte Brasil

Onto the local mountain of Angra do Heroísmo

Angra do Heroísmo – Monte Brasil and back

Starting point and destination: turismo in Angra do Heroísmo, 30m. Bus from Praia do Vitória and Biscoitos.
Walking times: Angra do Heroísmo – Monte Brasil ¾ hour, return ½ hour. Total time 1¼ hours.
Height difference: 175m in ascent and descent.
Grade: easy.
Refreshments: Angra do Heroísmo.

Time and time again in the Azores nature has performed big and small miracles which settlers could make use of. And so there are small, individual volcanoes to be found off some of the islands. Over a period of time sand and rock has been washed up to create a link with the island providing an ideal opportunity to build a small harbour town in the shelter of the local mountain. And so Angra do Heroísmo lies on the slopes of Monte Brasil, Horta on the slopes of Monte da Guia on Faial, and Velas on the slopes of Morro Grande on São Jorge. If you look carefully at the map, you will see that Monte Brasil is a small mountain range with 4 peaks: Pico do Zimbreiro, 198m, Pico do Facho, 205m, Pico das Cruzinhas, 168m, and Pico da Quebrada, 159m. Two craters which date from smaller eruptions can also be seen clearly.

From the turismo in **Angra do Heroísmo** go a bit further along the Carreira dos Cavalos down to the harbour and turn second right (Rua do Cons. Jacinto) into an undeveloped area. Now go uphill along an avenue to the Castelo do João Baptista which was in the 16th century an important fortification with castle moats, bulwarks, walls and ramparts. In the centre there's the 'São João Baptista' church, the governor's palace and the prison. Some units of the Portuguese army are stationed today in the Castelo. The church is no longer used and is now a memorial to freedom from Spanish rule. At the Castelo follow the road leading steeply up right as far as a picnic area with aviaries and a game enclosure. Where the path forks, turn right and go up through a countryside with tall heath bushes as far as the first viewpoint, the previously mentioned Pico do Facho – the highest point of **Monte Brasil**, 205m. From here there's an narrow tarmac road continuing up to the Relvão, also called Pico das Cruzinhas (mountain of the cross) where there's a pillar with a cross. Here is the best viewpoint over the town and the bay as far as Porto de Pipas (harbour of barrels) at the opposite end of the bay. In the south, the rock faces drop down vertically into the sea.

There are different versions of how Monte Brasil got its name. One says that Genoese sailors named it after brazil-wood. Rather more believable is the story about an emigrant who had become rich in Brazil and returned to buy the mountain which he named in memory of this country.

You can shorten your **return** by taking the direct route from Pico das Cruzinhas to the fort and to Angra do Heroísmo.

Fishermen at Angra do Heroísmo harbour.

17 From Furnas do Enxofre to Algar do Carvão and on to Angra do Heroísmo

Sights in the middle of the island

Furnas do Enxofre – Algar do Carvão – Angra do Heroísmo

Starting point: Furnas do Enxofre, 662m. Take a taxi (no buses).
Destination: Angra do Heroísmo, 30m.
Walking times: Furnas do Enxofre – Algar do Carvão ¾ hour, Algar do Carvão – Angra do Heroísmo 3¾ hours. Total time 4½ hours.
Height difference: 100 m in ascent, 730m in descent.

Grade: easy as far as the hydroelectric works, from there 200m of rather steep and difficult descent to the end of the water pipe and the first houses of Angra do Heroísmo.
Refreshments: Angra do Heroísmo.
Tip: you should allow an hour to visit Furnas do Enxofre and Algar do Carvão.

Furnas do Enxofre is little mentioned, but the fumaroles, the hot steaming sulphur springs, have something special to offer in this area of approximately 3 sq. km. Mosses grow in the sulphur springs and create a fascinating picture in the steaming landscape with their various tones of bright yellow to dark red. You can walk through the area on narrow paths and marvel at this unique scenery. It's amazing how these different luxuriant species of moss thrive in the hot water.

From **Furnas do Enxofre** descend a 600m long gravel path (at an altitude of 80m) until you come to a road. Continue left for 300m and then turn left again onto a gravel path. Follow this up for another 100 vertical metres to **Algar do Carvão**. In ½ hour you reach the entrance to the cave. (The cave is open from June to September from 14.00–16.00, but it would do no harm to ask at the turismo beforehand.)

The Algar do Carvão was declared a geologically protected site in 1987. Since 1963 the special involvement of the previously mentioned 'Os Montanheiros' has been with this unusual cave. The cave, about 100m deep, resulted from the cooling of the lava after a volcanic eruption about 2000 years ago. Huge stalactites and stalagmites have a variety of fantastic shapes and shades of colours. Fairly close to the entrance a volcanic chimney leads up vertically into the open air and is overgrown with luxuriant ferns and various species of moss. At a depth of 90m, the deepest place, there's a fresh water lake which has been formed from rain water. The depth in the middle is about 15m. Since the cave was electrified in 1988 you can climb down quite safely and see a full range of colour to black obsidian.

When you have left the grotto walk back along the ascent path back to the main road, keep right and after 300m you will reach a small wooden gate on the left-hand side.

Many species of moss thrive in the sulphur springs of Furnas do Enxofre.

Behind this over a hill covered in eucalyptus trees, you come to a narrow path marked with arrows. Continuing uphill through grassland for a short way you have a great view over the whole Caldeira de Guilherme Moniz, the largest crater of the archipelago. The diameter is about 15km, the crater rim is 150m high, the deepest point 458m. This enormous crater region is covered in thick moss and other plants.

With the caldeira on the left hand side continue walking along its rim to the elevation of Rosto with a geodetic surveying point. From here you have a marvellous view of the sea. The path goes past Japanese cedars, through meadows and pastures to a water reservoir at a crossroad.

Continue straight ahead. Walk along the 'Serra do Morião' and reach the next surveying point. It gives you a beautiful view of the coast in the south, the Serra da Ribeirinha, 410m, in the east the Serra do Cume, 545m, and in between, the pastures symmetrically enclosed with hydrangeas or dark stones which serve as motifs in all the leaflets on Terceira. With a bit of luck you will also see the Serra de Santa Bárbara, 1021m, the highest point of the island in the west which, for 300 days of the year, is so shrouded in cloud and mist that you can hardly see your hand in front of your face.

From this viewpoint descend to the hydroelectric works below.

Now leave the path which leads to the main road and take the narrow, rather difficult path which leads steeply down at the hydroelectric works. You come to some steps which descend next to the water pipes to the first houses, very steeply on the last 100m.

You come to the main road at a church. Follow this for a short way to the right until the road forks.

Go left to **Angra do Heroísmo**.

In Angra do Heroísmo's municipal park.

Pico, an island and a mountain

Pico, 2351m, is one of the highest mountains in the Atlantic and the highest mountain in Portugal and gave the island its name. You can travel either by ferry from Horta (Faial) to Madalena in just under half an hour or with SATA airline, also from Horta. The island has had an airport for a number of years. The sea between Faial, Pico and São Jorge is a wind tunnel. If the waves are higher than a one-storey house in the Azores, the ferry stops running. The airport closes when there's a wind-force of 12. All you can do is look through the hotel windows at the windswept scenery, which is a worthwhile sight except that the storm disappears as quickly as it arrives.

The crossing from Horta to Madalena with the 'Cruzeiro do Canal' goes past both the rocks rising out of the sea, 'Deitado' (the one lying) and 'Em-Pé' (the one standing). Between Pico and Faial there's a huge crater, 4km in diameter, below sea-level. The west of the island is dominated by Pico. Experts are expecting it to erupt in the course of the next 10,000 years and form its own caldeira. The lakes of Capitão, Caiado, Rosada, Paúl, Peixinho, Ilhéu and Negra are on the central plateau.

The vegetation consists of sparse undergrowth, cedars, laurel and brazilwood. The lava fields, called mistérios, which made the farmland infertile, lie strewn across the whole island and in places are densely wooded. The

The harbour of Madalena with 'Deitado' and 'Em-Pé' rocks .

Lagoa do Paúl in the highmountain area of Pico.

mistérios of Prainha, Santa Luzia, São João and Soldão are especially beautiful. On the plateau there are many small volcanic cones, the highest of which is Pico do Topo, 1007m, with grottoes and caves in which you can spend the night, if you want to climb Pico by today's less usual route.

The island of Pico has a problem with its mountain which sometimes causes amusement on Faial and São Jorge. If you live on Pico you have, on the rarest occasions, the chance to see Pico in its entirety without a layer of cloud. If you live on São Jorge or Faial you can see it much better and usually in the morning or the evening, enjoy the sight of it in all its beauty, with its various cloud formations too. The Azorean government has spent years studying these formations. An old mariner, Master Daniel from Horta, has established seven basic cloud caps and drawn conclusions from them about weather developments. These observations, 'The Hats of Pico', were published in summer 1996 in the 'Azores News'.

However the second largest island on the Azores has other things to offer apart from its mountain. Pico was the island of whalers until the ban on whale catching in 1987. People managed to live well from anything to do with it, from the building of boats to the industrial processing of whales. After the ban, a wave of emigration began and the population profile has been threatening to become older. Today a small boatyard in Santo Amaro makes boats by hand. There's a whale museum in Lajes do Pico. Whale

In Santo Amaro handicraft school.

watching is on offer at the Vigia da Queimada (whale watching station), a short walk from Lajes. Lajes is a very pretty village where you can stay over night at moderate prices.

Fishing plays a fairly large role on Pico as on the other islands. Almost all the villages which lie on the coast have a small harbour where the fishermen sit and the fishing boats are moored.

The villages on the west and south coast are lively with restaurants and cafés everywhere, while those on the east coast seem rather melancholy and tourists should take food with them because there are no facilities for refreshments.

There are no settlements in the interior of the island as there are on most of the other archipelago islands. The cultivation of fruit is also important for Pico. The lava soil, the sun and the climate bring about an abundance of all kinds of fruit. Early in the morning a 'fruit boat' transports certain fruit for sale to Horta.

Wine production is also important. The lava soil, the vines protected by walls of black stones, and the sun, especially on the south coast, enabled honey-sweet grapes to be grown by the first settlers. The famous Verdelho wine comes from these grapes and was already being exported centuries ago to Europe. There's also a light white table wine and the 'Vinho de Cheiro', a red wine which is a must at festival time. The fig schnapps is also highly respected and a sweet liqueur called 'Angelica'.

Festivals of the Holy Spirit are celebrated here as well of course. A special one is the 'Semana dos Baleiros' ('whale week') in Lajes in the last week in August, a religious festival with a picture of the saint 'Nossa Senhora de Lourdes'. Then there's a regatta with whaling boats, colourful processions, dancing, music and invitations to try the local food and wine.

A SUMMARY OF INFORMATION ABOUT PICO

Transport

Buses go right round the island on the coast road (time-table in the turismo). You can hire cars and bikes in Madalena.

Accomodation

Many tourists come just for a day, take a taxi round the island and return to Horta by ferry. If you want to stay longer you will get help with finding accommodation in the Madalena tourist office. There's also accommodation to be found in Lajes, Açor, Piedade and São Roque.

Grottoes and caves

Volcanic eruptions created grottoes and caves with many stalactites and stalagmites but also long underground passageways. A local guide and the necessary equipment are essential if you want to explore them.

18 Ascent of Pico

The highest mountain in Portugal and the most beautiful mountain in the Atlantic

Cabeço das Cabras – crater rim – inner summit of Pico and back

Starting point and destination: Cabeço das Cabras, 1200m. Take a taxi or hire a car (no buses). If you are coming from Madalena, drive along the main road towards the centre of the island. After 10km you pass the turn-off for Furna de Frei Matias, then after 3km turn right at a derelict building. After 5km you come to a car park with an information board about the nature reserve, the start of the ascent.

Walking times: Cabeço das Cabras – crater rim 2 hours, crater rim – inner summit (Pico Pequeno) 1 hour, descent 2¾ hours. Total time 5¾ hours.

Height difference: 1151m in ascent and descent.

Grade: difficult (for hikers), since 40 % of the ascent requires you to use your hands. Sure-footedness and a good standard of fitness needed. It's also advisable for hikers to take a guide with them. The turismo in Madalena will be able to arrange one for you. For experienced mountaineers this highest mountain in the archipelago will present no problems.

Refreshments: none.

Tip: if you are travelling by taxi, arrange the time you want picking up with the driver.

View from Pico das Caldeirinhas (São Jorge) of Pico at twilight.

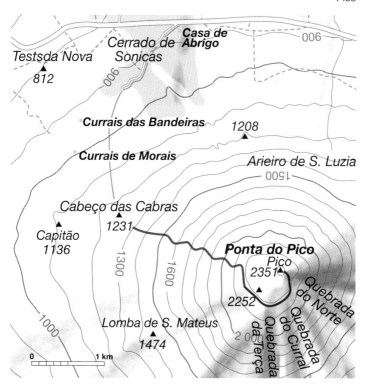

You should only go up Pico between June and September and in good weather. There are two ways of climbing Pico.

Either climb in the afternoon to be able to enjoy the sunset from the summit, then descend into the crater and camp there overnight (you can also sleep out in a cave). In the morning go up again to see the sunrise. In good weather this is an unforgettable experience. Take warm clothes and rain gear with you because it can be very cold on the top particularly when there's a break in the weather.

The easier alternative is to begin the climb at 8 in the morning, then you will be back at your starting point by 5 pm at the latest, even allowing time for the odd rest.

The start of the climb from the information board in **Cabeço das Cabras** is

Climbing Pico in bad weather.

not steep and the path is clear and well-trodden. The ground is overgrown here with heather and thyme. After 20 minutes you pass by a small crater. Continuing straight on you reach a waymarking post. It belongs to a series of waymarking posts which have been erected at a distance of 100m from each other by the Furna de Frei Matias. They date from the time when you began the climb in Furna de Frei Matias and the road didn't lead as far as Cabeço das Cabras. The posts are in urgent need of repair. In some places they have broken off and as the mists come up, they are difficult to find.

The path turns off left at the first post which is not easy to see, and then it goes steeply uphill forcing you to occasionally use your hands. There are no exposed places, but the path is sometimes covered in sand and small stones and there is a danger of slipping. In principle keep to the marked route since off the path there are cracks in the ground. There's more moss and undergrowth up to an altitude of about 2000m and the peak above is bare and steep.

When you have left the vegetation behind, allow another 30 minutes of steep and strenuous climbing, depending on your pace, to the **crater rim**.

Be prepared for the fact that the crater rim falls vertically down into the interior. The circumference measures 700m in all. Go carefully along the crater rim, watch out for scree, smooth slabs and fissures, and then you reach the entrance into the caldeira at the south-eastern edge. From the bottom of the crater you reach the **inner summit of Pico** (Pico Pequeno) which rises up 70m from the bottom of the crater at the northern edge of the caldeira. The last 100m of the climb are hard. But from the top you have a unique panorama.

Return back the same way to your starting point.

Pico, above low-lying clouds, from near Velas (São Jorge).

19 From Furna de Frei Matias to Madalena

On the slopes of Pico – pastures, fruit orchards and small woods

Furna de Frei Matias – Madalena harbour

Starting point: Furna de Frei Matias, 780m. Take a taxi (no buses).
Destination: Madalena harbour, 10m. Bus from Madalena along the coast road around the island.

Walking times: 2½ hours.
Height difference: 700m in descent.
Grade: easy.
Refreshments: Madalena.

As with so many places in the Azores there's a story about the Furna de Frei Matias cave. Before the arrival of settlers there was a monk by the name of Matias who lived here, a devout hermit still revered today. Previously this was the starting point for the climb up to Pico and that's why the arrows begin here.

Before the walk you should visit the cave in a lava field overgrown with grass. To reach this go along a gravel road from the main road, then through an iron gate and follow the arrow which leads you to the entrance to the middle cave. As with most of the caves in the Azores this one was caused by gas escaping in the cooling lava after a volcanic eruption. The cave stretches a long way, but the exact length is still unknown. The stalactites and stalagmites have been partly damaged by souvenir hunters.

Go from **Furna de Frei Matias cave** back to the main road, left along this and then after about 5 minutes turn right onto a narrow path. You come to a beautiful viewpoint with views of Madalena and over to Faial.

Continuing straight on you cross over the EN-3 main road 10 minutes after the viewpoint and then follow an old donkey path downhill between dark stone walls.

After half an hour you come to a light wood with evergreen trees and bushes. Before the settlers cleared the laurel woods, this side of Pico was densely covered in forest. What has remained serves today as protection for cattle against storms and rain.

On both side of the path you will find lots of the so-called 'moroiços' (piles of stones). The volcanic rock made the construction of fields impossible. The settlers worked hard to pile up the stones so that they formed low pyramids, the 'moroiços'. Today they look like dark spots on the countryside.

Cross over the En-3 again and 2 hours from the start of the walk you reach the first houses of the villages around Madalena and come onto a small road.

Going right, past a nondescript church, you come to the main road which goes round the island.

Turn left here and in 30 minutes, after you have reached the first houses, you arrive at **Madalena** harbour.

20 Coastal walk to Madalena

Impressive views of Pico, 'Deitado' and 'Em-Pé'

Monte – Calhau – Pocinho – Madalena

Starting point: Monte, 74m. Buses from Madalena and Candelária.
Destination: Madalena, 10m. Buses to Monte or Candelária, Lajes and Piedade.
Walking times: Monte – Pocinho just under ½ hour, Pocinho – Madalena a good 1½ hours. Total time 2 hours.
Height difference: 50m in ascent, 114m in descent.
Grade: easy.
Refreshments: restaurant above Calhau and Madalena.

Tip: in summer it's really hot, no shade. Take your swimming things.
Alternative: you can lengthen the walk by 1½ hours by starting in Candelária. Opposite the 'Nossa Senhora das Candelas' church take the small road to Porto de Ana Clara. Turn right there and go along an old link path through the hamlet of Fogo and a deserted village. After 40 minutes you come to the Ponta da Madre Silva isthmus and 10 minutes later Calhau. From here continue as described below.

If the weather doesn't seem good enough for a walk up to or around Pico you should take the opportunity of becoming familiar with the coast. The views are the special thing about this walk. On the left you can see Faial with the caldeira, usually enveloped in cloud. Pico towers up high on the right and in the foreground you approach 'Deitado' and 'Em-Pé', the rocks before the entrance to Madalena harbour.

From Monte to Madalena.

Monte, the starting point of this walk, is a picturesque little village with a windmill, narrow streets and old houses.

Go to the south end of the village and turn right into a narrow little street.

Walk leisurely downhill until you reach **Calhau**. The village comprises nine houses and has a small harbour. There's a restaurant a little way above on the hillside.

Leave Calhau to the north along an old donkey path which goes along the coast. On the left you can see the lava coast with deep inlets and on the right vineyards, which in some cases have grown wild.

You reach the old 'Pocinho' farmstead which is no longer cultivated. The sea is calm here and you can go down to the water to swim. The volcanic hill Pédo Monte, 135m, rises up behind the farmstead.

From Pocinho walk up to the main road at the north end of Monte village and for a short while stay on the road until a fairly broad path of red sand turns off left. There are vineyards on the left and right and small fig trees. The further you walk the nearer the path gets to the coast.

At the first houses of **Madalena** there are two possibilities. Either go along the roadway to the right or turn left down to the coast.

The latter path looking over the harbour could be beautiful, but unfortunately it has fallen into disrepair.

21 From Miradouro Terra Alta to Prainha

Where the north coast is at its most beautiful

Miradouro Terra Alta – Santo Amaro – Canto da Areia – Prainha

Starting point: Miradouro Terra Alta, 415m. Bus along the coast road all round the island.
Destination: Prainha, 20m. Bus along the coast road right round the island.
Walking times: Miradouro Terra Alta – Santo Amaro 1½ hours, Santo Amaro – Prainha 1½ hours. Total time 3 hours.
Height difference: 50m in descent.
Grade: easy. Path from Miradouro Terra

Alta to the coast can be slippery and covered in small stones. If you are not sure-footed, it's better to start the walk in the little village of Terra Alta.
Refreshments: bars in Santo Amaro and Prainha.
Tip: take your swimming things and allow time for a visit to the school of craftwork in Santo Amaro.

As with all the islands of the Azores it's rougher and more arid on the north coast of Pico than the south coast. The Miradouro Terra Alta, 415m, east of Santa Amaro is the most beautiful and highest viewpoint on the northern coast road. From here you have an impressive view of São Jorge.

From Miradouro Terra Alta a narrow, slippery path covered in stones leads down to the coast. At the coast turn left and follow the path past some old houses as far as **Santo Amaro**. You should take some time here to visit the Escola de Artesanato, the school of craft work. It was founded by two sisters and styles of craftmanship, which

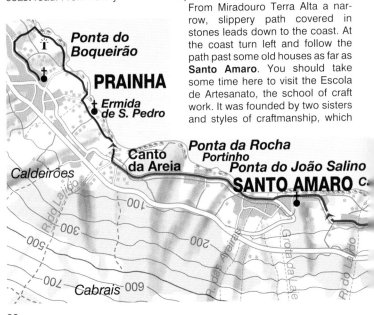

originated during the isolated life of the island, are being revived. Women and children learn how to make items of jewellery and flower arrangements from dyed fish scales. They learn how to spin, weave and knit, and how to produce traditional clothes, dolls from straw, straw hats and musical instruments. They learn the ancient art of willow-weaving, they make wooden articles which depict the scenes of daily life and make miniatures of whaling boats. Entry is free. You get a friendly welcome and are allowed to look at everything.

When you leave the school of handicrafts go past the church of baroque origin to the harbour. There's a boatyard here where boats are built as they were in the

Work from the school of handicrafts.

old days. Until 1983 boats were for catching whales, but now they are fishing boats. The path continues along the coast, past old farmhouses and new buildings.

Going gently uphill you come to the hamlet of **Canto da Areia**. Going downhill again you cross the Ribeira do Valado valley. A small bridge goes across and to the right and to the left there are vineyards and cornfields. On the right hand side there's a small chapel, the 'Ermida de São Pedro'.

After 1½ hours (from Santo Amaro) you reach Prainha. Continue along the coast to the lighthouse on the Ponta do Boqueirão. Past the ruins of a windmill and the sports ground you reach the sea-pool which is a nice place to have a swim.

From here ascend an tarmac path getting steeper to a T-junction, which you follow left to the centre of **Prainha**. As in many of the villages in the Azores there's a church here as well, the bus stop and a bar, and if you are getting picked up by taxi, the meeting place where the taxi will be waiting.

0   1 km

baixo da Rocha

rra   Pedra da   Ponta do
ta   Fonte   Espigão

Terra Alta

São Jorge, the island for hikers

Along the north coast.

56km long and up to 8km wide, São Jorge lies in the Atlantic like a fish. The island of Saint George is the fourth largest in the archipelago. Pico da Esperança, a mountain chain, runs along its full length and the highest point is 1053m. The main town and harbour is Velas. As Angra do Heroísmo lies on the slopes of Monte Brasil, so Velas lies on Morro Grande. The second largest town is Calheta, also situated on the south coast.

On both sides of the island, i.e. in the north and in the south, the coasts fall steeply away. The fajãs, plains which were transformed by the settlers into fruit orchards and fields, lie at sea level. Even dragon trees grow on many of the fajãs and tropical fruits thrive in this favourable climate. The fajãs of the Caldeira do Santo Cristo near Ribeira Seca are a special habitat and nature reserve with a grotto below sea-level and the only lake in the Azores in which they breed mussels.

Off the eastern tip of São Jorge lies the small Ilhéu do Topo where endemic plants still grow. Many seabirds breed here too. For this reason the island has been declared a nature reserve.

The shining green pastures with black and white spotted cows are an important source of income for São Jorge. From the milk they produce the queijo de São Jorge, the best cheese for miles around, a round cheese of 7 to 12 kilos in weight. It is dried in special rooms at an even temperature for a period of 3 months until it has a honey-coloured rind. This tangy cheese is exported to other countries because of its excellent taste.

Little is known about the settlement of the island. As on Santa Maria urzela (orchil) and pastel (woad) were exported to Europe for dyeing. Pirate attacks, food crises, earthquakes and volcanic eruptions hindered economic development as with the other islands in the archipelago.

But São Jorge remained somewhat behind São Miguel and Faial. The airport built in 1983 was already closed in 1986 – because of a lacking demand. Things have changed in the meantime. Word has got around with tourists that São Jorge is an ideal island for hiking. They have been arriving since then, albeit not in great numbers. Levada walking is the key word when talking about Madeira. Fajã walking might have an influence on the future of São Jorge. The 74 fajãs are quite different from one another and have a lot to offer the hiker.

Very important to the islands are the Festivals of the Holy Spirit: lively festivals with processions when even the cows are lavishly decorated and old songs are sung. Walkers are unhesitavingly invited to join in. The festival of Julho is the biggest event on São Jorge. Over 20,000 people get together in the town of Calheta for music, theatrical events, exhibitions and sporting festivities.

A SUMMARY OF INFORMATION ABOUT SÃO JORGE

Transport

There are buses between Velas and Topo, Velas and Calheta as well as Velas and ponta, but most of them are of little use to the hiker. A bus time-table and a list of taxi prices are available from the turismo in Velas. You can also find out from here where you can rent cars and mopeds.

Taxi drivers waiting at the airport replace the need for a tourist guide. They know their way around the island well and know what the tourists will find interesting. 'English spoken' is to be found on most of the taxis.

Accomodation

There are hotels and residencials in Velas, Calheta and Urzelina. A very modern hotel has been built on the coast at Velas which does not fit in at all with the Azorean style, but as recompense, Pico appears in all its glory at the breakfast table in the morning. There are, however, other comfortable residencials in Velas and information can be obtained from the turismo.

22 From Sete Fontes to the Farol de Rosais lighthouse and to Rosais

To the most beautiful viewpoint on the island

Sete Fontes forestry park – Farol de Rosais lighthouse – Rosais

The Farol de Rosais lighthouse.

Starting point: Sete Fontes forestry house, 380m. Take a taxi (no buses).
Destination: Rosais, 256m. Bus to Velas (three times a week)
Walking times: Sete Fontes forestry park – lighthouse 1 hour, lighthouse – Rosais 1¼ hours. Total time 2¼ hours.
Height difference: 98m in descent, 190m in ascent.
Grade: easy.
Refreshments: bars in Rosario.
Tip: a good walk to combine with Walk 23.

The Sete Fontes forestry park, the starting point for this walk, is very popular. On Sunday it attracts the locals to indulge in their favourite pastime, the picnic. Endemic and imported trees and other plants are to be found here, a children's playground and of course, a picnic area. There's also a small festival square with altar and little bell tower and a relief model of São Jorge island donated by the emigrants – everything just as the Azoreans like it. There's no restaurant, you bring your food with you. From here you can walk to the Farol de Rosais lighthouse, an interesting viewpoint.

When you come out of the **Sete Fontes forestry park** two paths turn off right. Take the one going diagonally right, a broad path with gravel and red sand, lined with bushes and trees. It goes leisurely downhill for 4km to the western point of the island. The **Farol de Rosais lighthouse** is here, surrounded by broken concrete slabs and metre-high reeds which you have to force your way through to reach the edge of the cliffs. The rock face falls 200m vertically down into the sea, a very beautiful, but also rather dizzy sight.

Go back to the lighthouse. In 1980 it was badly damaged by an earthquake (you can see the cracks in the tower), and has not been in use since this time. This earthquake whose epicentre was between São Jorge and Terceira also destroyed Angra do Heroísmo, the capital of Terceira. The entrance to the tower is securely locked for reasons of safety, but there are signs around which lead you to assume that this is also a popular picnic area.

The return goes 1km back along the same path at first, but then you follow a path off to the right which goes through an undulating landscape until you reach the first houses of **Rosais**, a long single-street village. At the village square, the centre of the village with 800 inhabitants, there's a bridge over the Ribeira da Agua. The church, an imperio, bars and a bus stop are all to be found in this square. This is where people meet and socialise. Perhaps you will be lucky enough to take part in a festival.

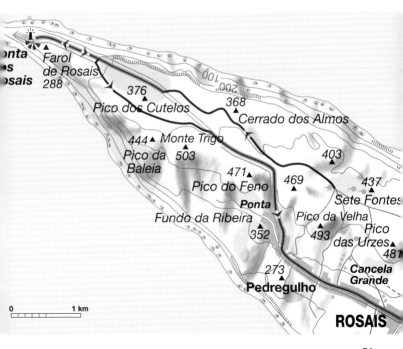

23 From Rosais via Serroa to Velas

The wilderness of São Jorge

Rosais – Serroa – São Pedro – Velas

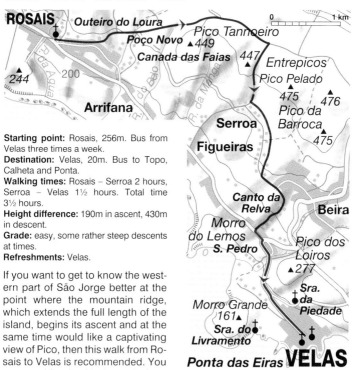

Starting point: Rosais, 256m. Bus from Velas three times a week.

Destination: Velas, 20m. Bus to Topo, Calheta and Ponta.

Walking times: Rosais – Serroa 2 hours, Serroa – Velas 1½ hours. Total time 3½ hours.

Height difference: 190m in ascent, 430m in descent.

Grade: easy, some rather steep descents at times.

Refreshments: Velas.

If you want to get to know the western part of São Jorge better at the point where the mountain ridge, which extends the full length of the island, begins its ascent and at the same time would like a captivating view of Pico, then this walk from Rosais to Velas is recommended. You can combine it with the walk from Sete Fontes to Rosais, and then it becomes a 6 hour walk, but not all that strenuous. Rosais owes its name to the St John's roses which blossom here in June.

At the church in **Rosais** a little street turns off and goes downhill between houses and gardens. After about 600m you turn left onto an tarmac road which after a short while turns into a path of red sand (there are quite a lot of these on São Jorge) and then above Pico Tannoeiro meets the road which runs along the spine of the island. Continue along this road, keeping Pico on your right at all times, and turn right after just under 1km onto a broad red path which goes downhill. The path goes through cattle pastures which are enclosed with blue hydrangea hedges from June onwards.

Before **Serroa**, which today only consists of deserted houses, turn left to Canto da Relva, a hamlet with a few houses, and continue downhill through Ribeirinho until you reach the EN-1 to **São Pedro**. The road divides here – left continues across the island, right goes downhill to Velas, past the sports field on the right hand side, and if you go right again you reach the Avenida do Livramento. A narrow path goes to the 'Nossa Senhora do Livramento' chapel at the foot of Morro Grande, but the Avenida goes straight on to **Velas**.

Festival of the Holy Spirit in Rosais.

24 Fajã do João Dias and Fajã do Centeio

To the most beautiful beach of São Jorge – an island crossing

Velas – Beira – Fajã do João Dias – Fajã do Centeio and back

Fajã do Centeio.

Starting point and destination: Velas, 20m. Bus from Topo, Calheta and Ponta.
Walking times: Velas – Beira ¾ hour, Beira – Fajã do Centeio 2½ hours, Fajã do Centeio – Beira 3 hours, Beira – Velas ¾ hour. Total time 7 hours.
Height difference: 800m in ascent and descent.

Grade: easy.
Refreshments: Beira und Velas.
Alternative: from Fajã do João Dias first return the way you came, then take the road branching off right to Rosais (1¾ hours). From here by taxi to Valas (buses only three times a week).

The pastures here in the west of São Jorge are bordered with hydrangea hedges which flower from June onwards and give this walk a special appeal. You can see Pico on the neighbouring island beyond.

You walk out of **Velas** along the road up left around Pico dos Loiros, 277m, then turn right and come to a narrow little road to **Beira**. On São Jorge, the island of the famous cheese, the biggest cheese factory is to be found in Beira. More than 50 cheeses, up to 12 kilos in weight, are produced in Beira every day. They mature for three months and are turned daily. If you are interested in visiting the cheese factory and possibly buying some cheese you are not likely to be turned away.

From Beira, walk a good kilometre along the road in the direction of Santo António and then turn left onto a gravel path. Continue along this for 3km until you reach a field path which branches off left. This field path finishes after about 200m in a meadow which you now cross over. On the other side, in the left-hand back corner of the meadow, begins a leisurely footpath to the fajã. At the fork in the path keep right. When you reach the coastline the path goes very steeply downhill round hairpin bends. The locals only visit this half-derelict little village and the beautiful white sandy beach of **Fajã do João Dias** at the weekend. It's a nice spot to take a break and have a swim.

A 200m long path goes from Fajã do João Dias to **Fajã do Centeio** where only one house is still lived in today.

Return the same way.

25 From Urzelina to Manadas

From a solitary church tower to the most beautiful church on the island

Urzelina – Casteletes – Terreiros – Manadas

Starting point: Urzelina, 25m. Bus to Velas and Calheta.
Destination: church in Manadas, 100m. Bus to Velas and Calheta.
Walking times: Urzelina – Terreiros 50min., Terreiros – Manadas 70 min. Total time 2 hours.
Height difference: 75m in ascent and descent.
Grade: easy.
Refreshments: none.

Urzelina is the liveliest village on the south coast and they've even adjusted to tourism here. The name comes from the urzela plant (orchil) whose dye was exported up until the 19th century. Due to its favourable position (on a sunny terrace, no steep mountains) fig trees, banana trees, palm trees and vines thrive in the gardens of Urzelina. The new twin-towered church seems huge. A popular motif for photos is the solitary tower of the old São Antonio church – the only thing to remain after the volcanic eruption which destroyed almost the entire village. Several windmills in red, blue and white stand out amongst the black lava boulders. At the small fishing harbour a bar has been set up in the remains of a fort. Old warehouses for storing oranges have been turned into holiday apartments and a small local museum, Exposição Rural, with crafts and items showing traditional customs. There's also an official campsite and a natural sea pool. Things are on the move.

Past the church in **Urzelina** you come to a red path which you take along the steep black coast towards Manadas. You have a view on the right hand side of Pico and Faial, on the left hand side of the mountain chain which runs the length of São Jorge.

After about 1.5km you come to the village of **Casteletes**. From here the route goes along the tarmac road via **Terreiros** to **Manadas**, past the 'Santa Rita' chapel. Behind the chapel turn right from the main street onto a small road. The cemetery is on the right, then there's a harbour and the most beautiful church on São Jorge, the Franciscan church of Santa Bárbara (founded in 1770). If it's closed, ask at the house in front for the key. The inside is magnificent, for the most part designed by local artists – only the azulejos come from Porto and the 12 pictures in the ceiling are by an Italian master. The reliefs in the ceiling are also very striking: Santa Bárbara, the patron saint for storms in the Azores, Saint George who gave his name to the island, and the dove as the symbol of the Holy Spirit who has great significance in the Azores. Carved wooden vines and leaves are a reminder of the local wine making.

The solitary church tower of Urzelina.

26 Over Serra do Topo to Fajã dos Cubres

To the fajãs on the north coast – the most beautiful walk on São Jorge

Field path turn-off – Caldeira de Cima – Fajã da Caldeira – Fajã dos Tijolos – Fajã do Belo – Fajã dos Cubres

Starting point: field path from the EN-2 between Calheta to Topo, 710m. Buses from Calheta and Topo. The field path branches off opposite a small concrete house and is clearly sign-posted from the road.

Destination: Fajã dos Cubres, 20m. Return by taxi (no buses). Arrange with the taxi driver on the way there when you want to be picked up in Fajã dos Cubres.

Walking times: field path turn-off – Caldeira de Cima 1 hour, Caldeira de Cima – Fajã dos Cubres 2½ hours. Total time 3½ hours.

Height difference: 80m in ascent, 770m in descent.

Grade: moderately difficult. Be ready for gusts of wind on the coast path.

Refreshments: none.

Alternative: from Fajã dos Cubres continue on the main road round hairpin bends to Norte Pequeno. 470m in ascent; 1 hour. The view back to the fajã makes a very beautiful photo. Some paths branch off left and right, but keep on the main path which at the end of the walk joins the main road of Norte Pequeno. Near the church there's a café. Buses from Norte Pequeno to Velas, Calheta and Topo.

This walk is clearly the most beautiful on São Jorge, if not one of the most beautiful in the Azores – and in the opinion of the manager of São Jorge's tourist office, an absolute must for every hiker who visits the island. When you are standing on the main road at the field path turn-off you will find yourself at a height of 710m and still on the south side of the island. If it's a bit foggy there's no reason not to do the walk as the weather is usually clear on the north side.

The **field path** goes gently uphill first of all for about 20 minutes until you have reached the highest point of the island's ridge. There's still pasture-land here. Then the path on the north side descends steeply and you look down almost vertically to the dark blue sea. The further you descend the more densely overgrown the path becomes with fern and sub-tropical plants, so that at times you have to force your way through. The gorge you are descending into is wonderfully wild. In the distance you can see the island of Graciosa.

Across a bridge you come to a couple of derelict houses and no people are to be seen anywhere about. **Caldeira de Cima** is no longer inhabited because it's too isolated.

Continue downhill and Fajã dos Tijolas with a few houses comes into view.

Before this you reach **Fajã da Caldeira**. The path meets a broader path here which goes across the hillside. The path goes up and down. As you come round the bends there's always another view and **Fajã do Belo** emerges with its derelict houses.

The path goes past two waterfalls which are usually dry in high summer. Then it descends to **Fajã dos Cubres** with a few houses, a small church and a lake.

São Jorge coastal scenery.

Serra do Topo.

27 From Fajã dos Vimes via Loural to Fajã de São João

Fajãs and steep coast – natural forests and luxuriant vegetation

Fajã dos Vimes – Fajã dos Bodes – Loural – Fajã de São João

Starting point: Fajã dos Vimes, 20m. Take a taxi via Ribeira Seca and Portal (no buses).
Destination: Fajã de São João, 20m. Return by taxi (no buses). Arrange with the taxi driver on the way there when you want to be picked up in Fajã de São João.
Walking times: Faja de São João – Loural, 1½ hours, Loural – Fajã de São João 2½ hours. Total time 4 hours.
Height difference: 480m in ascent and descent.
Grade: moderately difficult, at times rather steep ascents and descents.
Refreshments: none.

The eastern part of São Jorge's south coast has a lot to offer – sun and magnificent views, luxuriant forests with natural vegetation, steep coasts and fertile fajãs. The climate is so subtropical here that in protected places you will find the appropriate fruits and coffee plants.

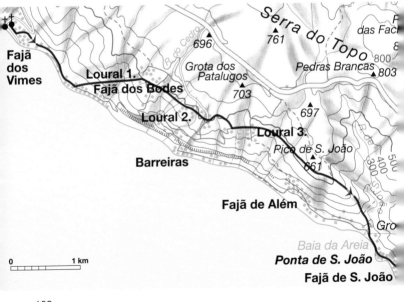

Descent to Ponta de São João.

A 4 hour walk from Fajã dos Vimes to Fajã do São João, including leisurely breaks, where you can count on the weather staying the same as it was at the start – this is one walk you should plan into your itinerary if time allows. Fajã dos Vimes is one of the largest fajãs on the island. The Ribeira dos Vimes which comes down from Serra do Topo flows through this fajã. The white houses, of which there are quite a few for a fajã, the fertile gardens, and the small harbour are cosily inviting and it's worth taking a short walk around.

Begin your walk at the church in **Fajã dos Vimes** and go along the coast to **Fajã dos Bodes**. The road ends when you have gone across the fajã. It turns into a path which follows the coast for a while, but then goes uphill into the mountains.

After 15 minutes on this path you reach a beautiful waterfall. Then there's a small meadow. 20 minutes later the path divides. Choose the left hand path which continues uphill.

After ½ hour you come to the first mountain houses and you see the three settlers' chapels of Loural which tower impressively over the coast. Loural stretches across the slope. Go over a road to the church and follow the path eastwards for about 700m.

The small road begins to wind downhill, sometimes a bit steeply. Keep left at the junction. You come to a paved donkey path and after 15 minutes pass by a waterfall. Now Fajã do Alem comes into view. Soon you will have reached the coast again at **Fajã do São João**.

Faial – hinting at the wider world

Faial, an irregular pentagon of 174 sq. km. with about 16,000 inhabitants, is one of the smaller islands in the Azores, but is one of the best known and most significant – with a very varied history.

The first person to have lived there was a hermit. The Flemish played an important role during the time of settlement and the name of the 'Flamengos' community is a reminder of that today.

Lying on the slopes of Monte da Guia the town of Horta and its harbour, today the capital of Faial, became an important intersection for trans-Atlantic ships. Trade flourished between political wars and pirate attacks. The Jesuits decided on Horta as a convalescence resort for missionaries from Brazil and the Orient and in the 17th century they built a large monastery. Whaling fleets used to moor in Porto Pim harbour in the 19th century to sign up new people – the Azorean sailors were much sought after because of their courage. After the quay was built in 1876 many ocean-going steamers came to refuel with coal.

In 1893 the first overseas cables were laid and in the first half of the 20th century Horta was the most important telegraphic communications centre.

Faial was the stopover point for the first trans-Atlantic flight. During the second world war Pan Am 'long-haul planes' landed there and the harbour became the base for the Allied Fleet.

The islands are well known for the Azores' high pressure which determines the weather in Central Europe. The meteorological station in Horta, from which weather data is sent to Europe and America, was named after Prince Albert of Monaco who was very interested in the Azores and the meteorological station.

Horta – seat of the Azorean parliament and the regional administration of tourism – is one of the most beautiful towns in the Azores: churches with magnificent paintings, São Francisco monastery, Santa Cruz fort and the museum with a valuable collection of ecclesiastical art. Of great importance is the marina – the harbour for ocean-going yachts from all over the world which have given the town a distinct character. The harbour wall of the marina is also an interesting sight for non-sailors. Every sailor who puts down anchor here, reaches for paint pot and brush to add another painting to the many pictures of varying styles which decorate the wall and the ground.

It is well known that seafarers are superstitious, and disaster is supposed to befall anyone who departs without leaving a painting. A notable gem is 'Peter's Café Sport' with its unmistakable blue façade. Sailors and other tourists meet here for a gin-fizz or to find help with a problem. You can buy souvenirs here, change money, look at the boldly decorated walls and marvel at the scrimshaw collection of elaborately carved whales' teeth on the upper floor. Also worth a visit is the Estalagem de Santa Cruz, a hotel and

The fortress of Horta has been turned into a good quality hotel.

restaurant. It was built into Santa Cruz fort, which dates from the 16th century, and covered in thick vegetation, it towers over the harbour.

Windmills and pastures, blue hydrangea hedgerows, hilly terrain, a varied coastline, small offshore islands, park-like scenery, villages close to the coast – the island of Faial has all this to offer. At 1043m Cabeço Gordo is the highest point and at the same time – in good weather – a marvellous viewpoint for the islands of Pico and São Jorge. The caldeira nearby, a crater of 2km in diameter and 400m deep, is covered in luxuriant vegetation so that the area has been declared a nature reserve. Even when the sun is shining down on the coast, the caldeira is frequently shrouded in thick mist. You need to be patient if you want to get to know it well.

There's a road round the whole of the island which the public bus service uses (time-table in the turismo of Horta). A rich abundance of plants grows on the north coast. A beautiful viewpoint is the Costa Brava, 320m, near Praia do Norte. The countryside around Norte Pequeno is characterised by rich green vegetation from which black lava rocks emerge up periodically. In the furthest west lies Ponta dos Capelinhos which was transformed by volcanic eruptions in 1957/58 into a futuristic landscape. On the south coast are to be found the thermal springs of Varadouro, with water containing salt at a temperature of 35.5 °C, ideal for anyone wishing to relax. Lajinha and Ponta Furada are also worth a visit with their caves and arches of lava rock and the sea surging around them.

28 A walk round the caldeira and descent into the crater basin

Wild nature, mostly shrouded in cloud or mist

Car park at the start of the tunnel – Cabeço Gordo – crater rim – tunnel – bottom of the caldeira – car park at the start of the tunnel

Starting point and destination: car park at the tunnel entrance to the caldeira, 900m. Take a taxi (no buses). Arrange with the taxi driver when to pick you up.
Walking times: walk round the crater rim 2 hours, descent into the caldeira and ascent 2 hours. Total time 4 hours.
Height difference: 460m in ascent and descent.
Grade: moderately diffi-

At the tunnel to the caldeira.

cult. Lack of vertigo and sure-footedness are required. Be careful: a piece of the outer flank subsided during the 1998 earthquake and it might be too dangerous to go round the whole rim. The descent into the crater is down a steep path.
Refreshments: none.
Tip: this walk can be combined with the descent from the caldeira to Horta (see Walk 29).

The walk round the Faial caldeira and the descent into its crater is the most beautiful walk on the island. However it's also the most uncertain area of the

View into the crater basin of the caldeira.

Azores as regards the weather. The caldeira is usually enveloped in cloud or the crater is lying in dense fog. You should only undertake the walk if you can see the caldeira clearly and even then you should be aware that clouds might suddenly appear.

There are some steps leading up from the **car park** at the left hand side of the tunnel entrance. After a short time you reach a geodetic surveying point and after that a steep path goes up some steps as far as the transmitter of **Cabeço Gordo**, 1043m. Depending on weather conditions you have a marvellous panorama from here of Faial and the neighbouring islands. Then follow a narrow tarmac road until it turns off left and continue straight ahead along a meadow path which runs along the **rim of the crater**. You reach a further geodetic surveying point and from here the path is at times only a narrow ridge. It's very steep down to the left and the right and you definitely need to have a good head for heights. There might even be some sudden gusts of wind which require you to keep a firm footing. In good visibility the views into the crater basin as well as into the distance beyond are unforgettable. Go round the rim of the crater and at the end you will come back to your starting point at the **tunnel entrance**.

If you go through the short **tunnel** (you'll need to duck!) you come to the interior of the caldeira. A steep narrow path to the right descends to the **bottom of the caldeira**. It's difficult and strenuous, but if you are interested in botany you should make the effort. The edges of the caldeira are at times wooded and in the bottom you will find small volcanic cones and two small lakes. The rest of the ground is overgrown with endemic shrubs and various species of moss – plants which love damp conditions.

The return to the **car park** at the tunnel entrance is back up the steep path.

29 From the caldeira to Horta

Pastures and endless hydrangea bushes

Car park at the caldeira – Casa do Guarda – Cruz do Bravo – Flamengos
Cruz do Bravo – Horta

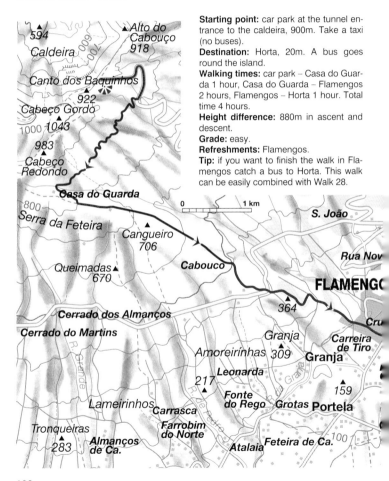

Starting point: car park at the tunnel entrance to the caldeira, 900m. Take a taxi (no buses).

Destination: Horta, 20m. A bus goes round the island.

Walking times: car park – Casa do Guarda 1 hour, Casa do Guarda – Flamengos 2 hours, Flamengos – Horta 1 hour. Total time 4 hours.

Height difference: 880m in ascent and descent.

Grade: easy.

Refreshments: Flamengos.

Tip: if you want to finish the walk in Flamengos catch a bus to Horta. This walk can be easily combined with Walk 28.

From the caldeira to Horta.

From the caldeira there are paths in all directions down to the coast. The route described here goes through fields and pastures which are enclosed by hydrangea hedgerows and offers wonderful views of the neighbouring island of Pico.

The walk begins at the **car park** at the tunnel entrance to the caldeira. First

of all it goes down the road until a gravel road bears right. Keeping roughly at the same height along here you cross over numerous streams.

After just under an hour the road bends to the left and shortly after that you come past the **Casa do Guardo**, a forestry administration building.

Now begins a lengthy stretch through the forest which consists mainly of Japanese cedars. The path is tarmac from here on and leads down over the Serra da

Feteira and past Cangueiro hill, 706m. Eventually it crosses the EN–1/2a. Continuing along the path you reach a crossroads in the street village of **Cruz do Bravo**. Left goes to **Flamengos**.

It's worth taking a detour into this friendly and picturesque village which lies idyllically in the Ribeira dos Flamengos valley. As the name already implies Flamengos goes back the earlier settlement by the Flemish and you shouldn't be surprised to see blond and red-headed children playing in the street. You will also see Flemish elements in the architecture. Due to its rather hidden location the village escaped the attacks by pirates in the earlier years.

Go back to the crossroads and continuing downhill to the left you soon come to the main road with a bus stop and an império (chapel).

Follow the road to the right. Monte Carneiro is on the left. With the mountain behind turn left into a narrow road which leads directly to **Horta**.

View of Cabeço Gordo.

The international meeting point, 'Peter's Café Sport' in Horta.

30 Monte da Guia and Caldeira do Inferno

View from the local mountain over the town and the island

Turismo in Horta – Monte da Guia – quay wall and back

Starting point and destination: turismo in Horta, 20m. Bus goes round the whole island.

Walking time: 1½ hours.

Height difference: 120m in ascent and descent.

Grade: easy.

Refreshments: bars and restaurants in Horta.

To get a view across the island, Horta and the harbour, it's worth taking a walk up the local mountain of Monte da Guia, 145m, at the start and looking down into the Caldeira do Inferno. Monte da Guia is connected to Horta only by an isthmus.

View into the Caldeira do Inferno from Monte da Guia.

The quay wall in the harbour at Horta with the pictures painted by sailors. It's said to be unlucky for a sailor not to leave a picture behind.

Begin the walk at the **turismo in Horta** diagonally opposite Fort Santa Cruz, walk past the marina to Porto Pim harbour and turn left towards the huge quay wall.

Past old warehouses and a disused whale factory you come to a road from the right which goes onto the northern flank of Monte da Guia. The road goes round two bends. The '**Nossa Senhora da Guia' chapel** is situated at the second bend.

Directly next to the chapel you can take a footpath up to the end of an isthmus which encloses the Caldeira do Inferno at the south. You have a beautiful view from here into the caldeira and Pico opposite. Monte da Guia has been declared a nature reserve because of the abundance of rare plants. Endemic plants thrive especially well on the caldeira slopes. You are urgently requested not to leave the paths or pull up any of the flowers.

The **return** is along the same path.

After the second bend when the road gets close to the beach, you can observe another small natural phenomenon. If a strong wave hits land a fountain shoots up out of a hole in the beach. Quite clearly at this point there is an underground connection with the sea.

Take the opportunity to go along the 370m long **quay wall** to look at the paintings made by the sailors.

31 From Lombega to Ponta de Castelo Branco and to Castelo Branco

Walk to an attractive viewpoint

Lombega – Ponta de Castelo Branco – Castelo Branco

Starting point: Lombega, 180m. There's a bus all round the island.
Destination: Castelo Branco, 60m. There's a bus all round the island.
Walking times: Lombega – Ponta de Castelo Branco 40 min., Ponta de Castelo Branco – Castelo Branco 80 min. Total time 2 hours.
Height difference: 110m in ascent, 230m in descent.
Grade: short walk, but a lack of vertigo is necessary. Steep ascent and descent at Ponta de Castelo Branco. The descent can be slippery.
Refreshments: Castelo Branco.
Alternative: with swimming things in your rucksack take a detour to the sea – about 30 min. there and back. From Castelo Branco go about 200m along the main road towards Horta and then walk downhill to the right on the Caminho do Porto. You reach the fishing harbour and below the airport a picnic site with toilet facilities, a snack-bar and a natural sea-pool. A beautiful place for swimming.

The walk is not demanding and doesn't offer any unusual or special features, but is enjoyable if you want to visit the typical villages of Faial and you like interesting views.

From Lombega to Ponta de Castelo Branco.

Lombega, the starting point for this walk, is pretty and picturesque and worth a few photos. At the western end of the village turn left onto a hiking path which goes leisurely down to the coast through fields with small trees. Your first objective is the volcanic cone of **Ponta de Castelo Branco** (white castle), 148m, a light-coloured rock on top of a dark grey plinth which is joined to the deeply indented coastline by a narrow land-bridge. For the land-bridge and the subsequent steep climb you need a good head for heights. Once you've arrived at the top of Ponta de Castelo Branco there's a beautiful view of the steep coastline to Varadouro, to Monte da Guia and of course, because we are on the south coast, of Pico which dominates everything around. Many sea birds breed on the ponta and there's talk of closing it off.

You should take your time on the descent, being careful not to slip. Eventually you walk along a track near to the coast through cattle pastures and cornfields in the direction of Castelo Branco. Then you leave the coastal path to the left and meet the main road. Follow this to the right as far as **Castelo Branco**.

Faial

32 From Capelo to Capelinhos

Walk into an eerie desert landscape

Capelo – Vale Formoso – Capelinhos

Starting point: Capelo, 170m. Take a taxi (no buses).
Destination: Capelinhos, 27m. Return by taxi (no buses).
Walking times: Capelo – Vale Formoso 25 min., Vale Formoso – Capelinhos 35 min. Total time 1 hour.
Height difference: 143m in descent (170m as far as the bay).
Grade: easy, possibly through deep sand.
Refreshments: none.

Alternative: if you are fascinated by the landscape you can walk from Capelinhos to Norte Pequeno in 1 hour. Return by taxi.
Tip: in Canto visit a small volcano museum with explanations of the volcanic eruptions in the area as well as photos and samples of rock and lava. A leaflet 'Capelinhos Volcano' is available in English from the turismo in Horta. Take your swimming things with you for a swim in Capelinhos bay.

Ponta dos Capelinhos cliff.

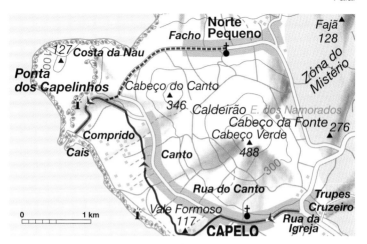

The futuristic landscape of Capelinhos at the north-western tip of the island is a special feature of Faial. This totally bare landscape with a steep, sheer coastline has a strange attraction. Between the 27th September 1957 and the 24th October 1958 there were about 200 volcanic eruptions and earthquakes. They were small, but registered up to 10 on the Richter scale and they completely altered the landscape and considerably increased the size of this end of the island. In Capelinhos the glowing lava was propelled into the air up to a height of 500m. The caldeira responded with steaming fumaroles and most of the lake in its crater basin disappeared into fissures. More than 300 houses were destroyed in Praia do Norte, and the little village of Camprido almost completely. Only the Capelinhos lighthouse remained intact while the surrounding fields were covered in ash, metres thick. What remained was an eerie landscape which has also been the backdrop for the shooting of a futuristic film. If you want to explore the landscape, choose a day without wind because otherwise it can be very unpleasant when the sand swirls up.

In **Capelo** turn off left at the blue and white imperío and head towards the coast to the hamlet of **Vale Formoso**. Here you come to a broad path of red sand which leads through a countryside with interesting flora. After just under half an hour you have reached the **Capelinhos** lighthouse and can see the enormous Ponta dos Capelinhos cliff.

The further you walk into this landscape between the bright yellow to black sand-dunes, the more remains of houses you will see that have been destroyed.

Graciosa – for walking and relaxing

With its 61 sq. km. Graciosa is, after Corvo, the second smallest island of the Azores. It is also the flattest and the one with the best weather. The highest point is on the rim of the caldeira, 402m, and the highest mountain is Pico Timão, 398m. A look at the map shows you that the island is not only inhabited all the way round the coast, but also in beautiful places in the island's interior. Many paths therefore criss-cross the island through soft, green undulating countryside and all of them end in the beautiful main town of Santa Cruz da Graciosa.

The airport was built in the 1980s and it arouses general interest when a few tourists get off the plane. Graciosa is not a touristy island. Only a few Azores fans stray here at the most, having heard or read about the Furna do Enxofre (sulphur caves). So the island is still a bit sleepy and people walk a trifle slower than anywhere else.

Graciosa was previously a prosperous island. Barley, corn, wine and the popular Graciosa brandy were exported, but under the rule of Salazar (1932 to 1968) progress passed it by. Primarily in the 1960s, 7000 of the 12,000 inhabitants emigrated to the USA and to Canada, since there were no opportunities for further education but by and large the elderly stayed on.

Santa Cruz da Graciosa is a bit too large for the main town of the island. There are three hotels, Flori's cocktail bar, the friendly meeting point, and the Discoteca Moinho (mill disco). Rossio is the main square, and even this is too big. Its real name is 'Largo Fontes Pereira de Melo'.

Here are the town hall, the court, the taxi rank, a band stand for the brass band, cafés and one of the typical round buildings which houses the tourist office in the main squares in the Azores. There are no regular opening times. If it's closed it's best to go into the town hall opposite and get your information there.

Beautiful, large araukaries give the square some shade. The old men sit on benches underneath and chat. Two big green water tanks and houses of distinguished Azorean families complete the picture.

A few steps away from the square is the imposing Igreja Matriz (the parish church) with a magnificent gilded altar and striking wooden statues in the side chapels. Around the year 1700 the Third Order of Franciscan monks built a big church behind the Rossio which fell into ruin in the 19th century and only a small tower survived as a symbol and has been decorated with azulejos.

A small museum of folk art (Casa Etnográfica) has been set up in a Celtic house and with serious commitment, the collection is regularly added to. Alga is dried for export in the harbour. The ferries from Horta on Faial do not dock here, but go further south into Praia harbour. But it's not a busy service.

Leisurely farm tracks tempt the hiker.

33 Monte Ajuda

To the three hermit chapels on Santa Cruz da Graciosa's local mountain

Rossio – Monte Ajuda and back

Starting point and destination: Rossio (central square in Santa Cruz da Graciosa), 9m.
Walking times: Rossio – Monte Ajuda 1 hour, return ½ hour. Total time 1½ hours.
Height difference: 120m in ascent and descent.
Grade: easy.
Refreshments: Santa Cruz.
Tip: before you start the ascent, ask the priest of Santa Cruz (everybody knows him) for the key to the 'Nossa Senhora da Ajuda' chapel.

If you look around the Rossio, the main square of Santa Cruz da Graciosa, you will first notice the town hall, the two water tanks and the parish church behind. Then your gaze goes up to a green undulating countryside with a mountain, enhanced by three chapels, just outside the town.
There are already signs at the **Rossio** which point the way to a beautiful footpath leading up this mountain.

The inordinately large town hall on the Largo Fontes Pereira de Melo (Rossio).

View from Monte Ajuda at Santa Cruz.

Follow the 'enhora da Ajuda' path and ascend the leisurely path 120m up the south slope until you reach the **Monte Ajuda** car park. The strange sight greets you of the three Ermidas (hermit chapels).

Turn off left onto the track to the 'São Salvador' chapel and then continue to the 'São João' chapel.

Back at the car park continue to the 'Nossa Senhors da Ajuda' chapel, the most important of the three. It was built in the 16th century and from the outside looks more like a fortress. The beautiful azulejos pictures in the interior date from the 18th century.

From here at the top there's a wide view of Santa Cruz da Graciosa, the airport on the left of it and afterwards the northern part of the island with its vineyards, which is less interesting to the walker than the southern part. You can also see a row of 24 windmills with their shining red domes, the symbol of Graciosa. A large part of the windmills has today fallen into disrepair. In August you can watch the bullfights from Monte Ajuda which are part of the 'Cristo dos Milagres' festival.

From the 'Nossa Senhors da Ajuda' chapel a cobbled road leads past a small bullfight arena and joins the path which you came up on. Return on this to the **Rossio**.

34 Round walk from Santa Cruz via Dores and along the coast

Vineyards, windmills and the roar of the sea

Santa Cruz da Graciosa – Dores – windmill – Santa Cruz da Graciosa

Starting point and destination: Rossio (central square of Santa Cruz), 9m.
Walking times: Santa Cruz – Dores 1¾ hours, Dores – Santa Cruz 2¼ hours. Total time 4 hours.
Height difference: none.

Grade: easy walk. Sometimes you need to climb over a vineyard wall and now and then walk along it.
Refreshments: bars and restaurants in Santa Cruz.

From the Rossio, the central square in **Santa Cruz da Graciosa**, walk along the street where the taxi rank is, northwards out of town.

Almost at the end of the town you come past the Residencial Graciosa, an old wine cellar which was converted tastefully into a 16 bedroom hotel (without restaurant). Its exterior is exactly in keeping with the style of Santa Cruz houses, two-storeys, shining white with black painted doors and shop windows. The pantiles are red.

Go past the turn-offs to Guadalupe and Vitoria on the left and continue straight ahead. After 2km turn off right to **Dores**, then go left through the village and right, past a small chapel.

Continue through the village until you come directly to a path that leads through vineyards. The small fields are enclosed with small stone walls in Azorean vineyard style and the landscape has a chequer-board appearance. Then a white **windmill** emerges up ahead with a red domed top. The windmills in the Azores, with the exception of the Corvo windmills, all look the same. They are supposed to be of Flemish origin, but it's not certain if that's true.

Go on the path round the windmill to the right and after 200m you come to a large semi-circular tower where the path finishes. There are some old vineyards in front which are now overgrown with ferns. With a bit of skill you can climb over the walls. Keep heading north-westwards. Sometimes you need to make a big step from one wall over to another, but this 'wall-walking' is not difficult.

After about 30 minutes it finishes and you come to an uncultivated field which you go across. Another 15 minutes and you reach the roadway which goes round the coast. If you cross over this road you reach the path on the other side behind some bushes between the road and the sea.

Walk along the beach round a wide bend, come to a picnic area and continue until the beach gets more and more narrow and finally huge waves and big lava boulders force you to return along the road to **Santa Cruz da Graciosa**.

Windmills and vineyards on the round walk via Dores to Santa Cruz da Graciosa.

35 Furna do Enxofre and round the caldeira

A geologically unique sulphur cave

Car park – Furna do Enxofre – round the caldeira – Can Longa

Starting point: car park before Furna do Enxofre, 137m. Take a taxi (no buses).
Destination: Can Longa, 130m. Return by taxi (no buses).
Walking times: descent into Furna do Enxofre and back up 2½ hours (including a visit to the cave), round the caldeira and descent to Can Longa 1 hour. Total time 3½ hours.
Height difference: 180 steps to Furna do Enxofre. 80m in ascent and descent round the caldeira.
Grade: easy.
Refreshments: none.
Alternative: descent from the crater rim

on a narrow track through some fields to Fenais and from there a walk along the coast to Praia. There's a small restaurant here.
Tip: the entrance to the cave is locked. Normally in the summer months the door-keeper is there to let you in. If, however, you should find the door locked because no tourists are expected, the taxi driver will know what to do. Everyone knows the keeper of the key and it's easy to find him. You should visit the cave between 11.00 and 14.00 when the sun is shining into the cave and the light conditions are better.

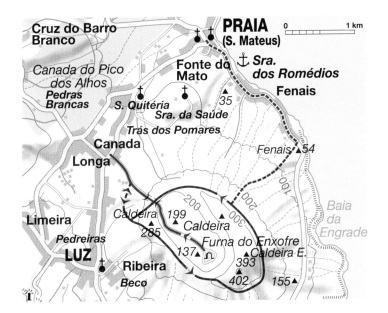

Typical farmhouse on Graciosa.

The 'Furna do Enxofre' cave is an exceptionally rare volcanic phenomenon and if you want to believe the scientists, geologically unique. Its vault is large, 80m high, 220m long and 120m wide. There's also a lake about 130m in diameter and up to 15m in depth. The water contains sulphur. Prince Albert of Monaco, an important ocean explorer in the 19th century, was one of the very first visitors to the cave. In 1879 he descended a rope ladder. In 1939 the descent was made easier and a shaft was constructed with 180 steps.

From the car park before **Furna do Enxofre** go to the entrance of the cave and down the 180 steps. At the bottom you will be amazed at the unique character of this massive cave. To the left you can continue a short way beside the lake until you come to a rope. You're not allowed any further and anyway, a longer stop is definitely not advisable because of the sulphur fumes. After you reach daylight again you can stop for a rest at the nearby picnic area or take a walk through the caldeira to look at the bold landscape and the crater slopes.

Then go through the tunnel out of the caldeira. 100m behind the tunnel you come to a footpath branching off left. Go along this to reach the **crater rim**. You now walk along a wonderful path around the caldeira on the outside. Alternating views present themselves of the coast and the sea and the glistening island in its many shades of green.

After about 1 hour you come back to the ascent path which you follow to the right until you meet the approach road to the rim of the crater. Turn left to **Can Longa**.

Flores, the island of flowers

A lake in the interior of the island.

Along with Corvo, Flores belongs with Corvo to the western group of islands. With its 142 sq. km. it is one of the smaller islands of the archipelago. The highest mountain is Porro Alto, 914m. The varied landscape goes from deep valleys carved by streams, over mountains, interesting rock formations and undulating countryside to the tips of isthmuses and coastlines which fall away into the sea.

The island got its name from the luxuriant abundance of plants and flowers. If you look at a map you will find that the villages lie around the coast and the interior is not inhabited. There are instead seven lakes in volcanic craters with narrow sandy banks and surrounded by hydrangeas. On the west side many waterfalls plunge down into the depths, sometimes several hundred metres.

The main town of Santa Cruz das Flores is not particularly attractive. It's lacking in flair and atmosphere which make the other islands so friendly. The people are not as happy and open either, but appear rather indifferent. If you come form Horta (Faial) you will notice the difference more acutely. Just outside near the airport there are two newer hotels, one with a restaurant and the other boring and totally lacking in charm. Apart from that there are two other simple hotels in town and you can also rent rooms privately. If you are looking for accommodation you can ask the taxi driver, or in a restaurant or grocer's. Also a visit to the turismo is very useful. Only a few tourists come to Flores, mostly those who have been several times to the Azores and now want to become acquainted with the western islands. Usually they stay one night in Santa Cruz and then go on to find a place to stay in Lajes or Ponta Delgada.

The west coast of Flores is a walker's paradise. If you have come chiefly to walk it's better to find accommodation there. There are beds in Lajedo and in Fajã Grande. Otherwise you will have to content yourself with a tent. There are already some sign-posted hiking paths on Flores.

And now we're on the subject of transport. It's best to travel by taxi and make the usual arrangements about when and where to be picked up.

You can rent a car only in Santa Cruz. On Mondays, Wednesdays and Fridays there's a bus at 08.00, and in winter at 09.00, from Fajã Grande through the villages to Lajes. From there you can get a connection to Santa Cruz. The return from Lajes to Fajã Grande is at about 15.00.

Then there's also the milk lorry which collects the milk in the Lajes area and takes it to Santa Cruz. It will stop if anyone flags it down at the side of the road.

View of Lajedo in the south-west of Flores.

36 From Santa Cruz to Ribeira da Badanela

A wonderfully wild valley with striking basalt rock formations

Santa Cruz das Flores – Monte – Fazendas de Santa Cruz – Ribeira da Badanela and back

Starting point and destination: Hotel Occidental at the airport north of Santa Cruz das Flores, 30m. Take a taxi (bus in the morning from Lajes to Santa Cruz).
Walking times: Santa Cruz – Fazendas de Santa Cruz 1 hour, Fazendas de Santa Cruz – Ribeira da Badanela 1 hour, return 1¾ hours. Total time 3¾ hours.
Height difference: 280m in ascent and descent.
Grade: easy.
Refreshments: Santa Cruz and restaurant at the entrance to Fazendas de Santa Cruz.

The church at the start of the Ribeira da Badanela valley.

This walk is ideal for familiarising yourself with the country and the people on Flores. It begins at the Hotel Occidental, one of the two big hotels in close proximity to the airport north of **Santa Cruz**. Go past this hotel on the right on the seaward side. There's a fish restaurant on the left and on the right a disused whale factory. Continue as far as the road, then go up some old stone steps on the right between fishermen's houses and lots of flowering watercress, rather steep but not dangerous. At the end of the steps you come to **Monte**. Do not be put off by the noisy barking of dogs on all sides. The roofs of the houses are secured with stones. Flores is the windiest of the Azores islands.

The walk continues along the road by the coast, past Ponta do Capitão to **Fazendas de Santa Cruz**. If you look out to sea you will see the island of Corvo with Vila Nova do Corvo and if you look inland, an impressive church rises up on a small mountain before the start of the Ribeira da Badanela valley, a beautiful sight from all sides. Fazendas de Santa Cruz, not to be confused with Fazenda near Lajes das Flores in the south of the island, is a street village which extends into the valley. At the end there's a picnic area with a trout pond.

Cross over a small reservoir and then continue walking along the path on the right hand side into the **Ribeira da Badanela** valley. You will see basalt rock formations on the sometimes very steep valley walls. The view back to the church situated at the start of the valley and the glistening sea is impressive. Sometimes the path cuts its way through the undergrowth, sometimes it's overgrown with grass, and it alternates between a steep and gentle incline. After about 1 hour from the picnic area the path ends in a pasture and there's a magnificent view of the steep wooded valley slopes of the Ribeira da Badanela with the striking basalt rock formations.

The **return** is back along the same path where you can enjoy views of the church and the sea.

37 From Lajedo to Mosteiro

To the basalt needles of Rocha dos Bordões

Lajedo – Rocha dos Bordões – Mosteiro and back

Starting point and destination: Lajedo, 200m. Take a taxi (no buses).

Walking times: Lajedo – Mosteiro 1 hour, return 1 hour. Total time 2 hours.

Height difference: about 125m in ascent and descent.

Grade: easy.

Refreshments: bar and small shop in Lajedo. In the shop you can also buy coffee and ice-cream. It's open on weekdays from 14.00 to 17.00 and Sundays after mass.

Alternative: you can combine this walk with the one from Fajãzinha to Fajã Grande (see Walk 38).

Lajedo lies at the south-western tip of Flores in a green valley between rocks and mountain ridges. It was previously a potters' village, but these times are over and today people live off the land.

There are two paths from Lajedo to Mosteiro, one upper, one lower. The lower path is the one to be recommended. It leads across the hillsides and offers a beautiful view of the sea and the Rocha dos Bordões. This huge rock is the symbol of the island, a geological phenomenon, created by the hardening of the basalt in high vertical pillars which today form the plinth of the massif. At the foot of the Rocha, boiling sulphur springs bubble in small holes, the 'Aquas Quentes'.

In **Lajedo** you first follow the path a short way towards the harbour, descend to a stream and cross over a stone bridge with two arches. Then continue uphill again and straight on past **Rocha dos Bordões**.

You can, of course, go and see the sulphur springs at the Rocha.

Behind Rocha dos Bordões the path goes uphill until you reach the small village of **Mosteiro** (65 inhabitants), just above the church. The church, built in 1846, has an old statue of Saint Filomena, which Antonio des Freitas, the founder of the church, brought with him from Macao. His son was the writer, Antonio Maria de Freitas, who died in 1864 in Santa Cruz.

Go **back** along the same path where you will be able to view Rocha dos Bordões from its especially photogenic side.

The basalt needles of Rocha dos Bordões.

38 From Fajãzinha to Fajã Grande

A special landscape characterised by waterfalls

Fajãzinha – Fajã Grande and back

Starting point and destination: Fajãzinha, 120m. Take a taxi (no buses).
Walking times: Fajãzinhas – Fajã Grande 1 hour, return 1 hour. Total time 2 hours.
Height difference: just under 150m in ascent and descent.
Grade: easy.
Refreshments: in Fajãzinha there's a shop in which you can also get coffee, drinks and ice-cream. Bar in Fajã Grande.
Alternative: you can combine this walk with the one from Lajedo to Mosteiro (Walk 37). Continue to Mosteira as described in Walk 37, then on the road to Fajãzinha and as below, to Fajã Grande (altogether 3 hours). The middle section (from Mosteiro to Fajãzinha) isn't particularly interesting and goes through cattle pastures.

The location of Fajãzinha and Fajã Grande, the western point of the island and Europe too, is unusual. The shoreline is flat, and the precipice over which waterfalls cascade, goes along behind the villages. The fajã is fertile and there are vegetable and fruit gardens. You will also find old windmills. If you climb onto the plateau up through the rock face you will discover four large crater lakes: Lagoa Funda da Fajãzinha, Lagoa Comprida, Lagoa Branca and Lagoa Seca.

In order to walk from **Fajãzinha** to Fajã Grande take the path a little to the right in Fajãzinha towards the two small windmills and cross over the stream (Ribeira Grande) at a suitable place. If there are problems use the new bridge further up where the road goes over. On the other side of the stream a narrow path continues up the hillside and the last houses of Fajãzinha disappear from view. At the end of

132

the ascent you come to a spring, then the broad path goes downhill to **Fajã Grande**. Since 1954 the houses of Fajã Grande have had running water and not until 1970 did they also get electricity. The number of inhabitants has greatly decreased through emigration. There are still two fishing boats and the fine sand from the shoreline is used for building. On the beach they have fitted out a building with a bar, restaurant, showers and toilets – a very beautiful place for a swim and, especially in summer, a wonderful place to enjoy the sunset.

At the waterfalls between Fajãzinha and Fajã Grande.

Corvo, the smallest of the islands

Corvo, the most northern and the smallest of the islands in the archipelago, is something special. It only has one town, one street and one policeman. If you get as far as the west of the Azores you should definitely make a visit to this island with its decidedly hospitable inhabitants, and not a one-day flying visit at that. Three days with travel there and back are just about right.

If you look across from Flores you see a small, thick lump in the sea, which was catapulted high up into the air two million years ago from a volcano – 17 sq. km., with 15km of coastline, dropping nearly 500m steeply down to the sea in the north and in the west.

Corvo is very windy and it is supposed to rain 300 days in the year, but that's not an official figure. The only road, covered in tarmac since 1996, leads up to the caldeira, called caldeirão here, an enormous crater, 3400m in circumference and 300m deep with two lakes. The highest point of the island is Morro dos Homens, 718m. There are 1100 cattle and 50 semi-wild horses on the island.

Vila Nova do Corvo is the name of the town where everything takes place. With 320 inhabitants it is the smallest Portuguese island with town privileges, a policeman and a town hall in which there's a lot going on and where the mayor himself advises the tourists. His only worry is the 360 mostly agricultural vehicles which rattle round the island, droning and horns beeping.

It's very lively in Vila Nova do Corvo. There are two restaurants, a café, a bar, children, dogs and chickens in the narrow streets and countless cats which clearly all have the same grandfather. Apart from private rooms you can enquire in the restaurant or the town hall about accommodation. There's also a small residencial at the end of the village with six rooms, nice, friendly and cosy.

Vila Nova do Corvo consists of four narrow streets. The washing on the roofs flaps in the breeze. Pedestrians and cars cannot get past each other in the streets and pedestrians have to somehow squeeze of the way. It's difficult when you want to buy something, as none of the shops have a shop window or a sign of any kind. So then you have to ask someone and a chain curtain is opened and you're standing in a shop. If you speak a bit of Portuguese you are a welcome guest, because Corvians love company. They have a very sociable relationship with one another and are related to each other in some way. So the doors have no locks. The patron saint of Corvo is 'Nossa Senhora dos Milagres' whose statue is worshipped in the church of the same name. It dates from a Flemish master from the beginning of the 16th century.

Corvo has had an airport since 1993 where a small SATA plane lands three times a week. A ferry boat of Senhor Augusto, the most important man of Flores, goes between Flores and Corvo in the summer, a service for vehicles and tourists. In other words you can travel in the morning from Flores to Corvo in 1½ hours, use the taxi service up to the caldeira which the Corvo community have specially organised, quickly take a few photos from the top and travel back to Flores again by boat.

Although in this way, of course, it's obvious that you hardly get a real impression of Corvo.

View of Vila Nova do Corvo with the airport runway and the island of Flores in the background.

39 From Vila Nova do Corvo to the caldeira

The smallest island and a big crater – an unforgettable walk

Vila Nova – Coroa do Pico – Espigãozinho – crater floor and back

Starting point and destination: church in Vila Nova do Corvo, 40m.
Walking times: Vila Nova – Espigãozinho 2½ hours, Espigãozinho – crater floor ½ hour, crater floor – Espigãozinho 1 hour, Espigãozinho – Vila Nova 2 hours. Total time 6 hours.

Height difference: 730m in ascent and descent.
Grade: easy walk on tarmac road as far as the Espigãozinho viewpoint. Descent into the crater over cushioned moss.
Refreshments: restaurants in Vila Nova.

Vila Nova do Corvo in the evening light.

Since 1996 the road in Vila Nova do Corvo to the Espigãozinho viewpoint, from which you can look down into the crater, has been completely surfaced – less of a joy to the hiker, but for farmers who work their fields here a great advantage. If you don't fancy the tarmac road you can ask in the O Caldeirão restaurant in the airport when the local mini-bus goes up. It's also quite sensible to look and see if there's anything brewing in the caldeira.

From the church in **Vila Nova do Corvo** go up the narrow street out of the village. After two big hairpin bends go leisurely uphill.

After 30 minutes you reach the Calçadas haystack – there are no more houses here. The path continues past cornfields, vegetable gardens and cow pastures, all of them enclosed in Azorean fashion with walls. Then you cross the Ribeira da Lapa and the Ribeira do Cerrado after that.

At **Coroa do Pico** you come to a fork. Go left here, at first quite steeply uphill, and then the last part as far as **Espigãozinho** less steeply again. The viewpoint is at 598m. In good weather you have a wonderful view of the crater rim and down into the caldeira with the two lakes 170m below. The crater rim reaches a height of 700m in the south. On the slope opposite there are more cornfields and vegetable fields enclosed by stone walls. On the left of the viewpoint a path goes down to the 2 km wide **crater floor**. It goes through damp meadows and over moss. But if the weather is reasonably good you should enjoy the descent from 598m to 427m and let yourself be impressed with the atmosphere.

Then return back along the same path to **Vila Nova do Corvo**.

40 To the north-east coast of Corvo

Whale watching and bird watching

Vila Nova do Corvo – Coroa do Pico – Canto da Carneira and back

Starting point and destination: Vila Nova do Corvo church, 40m.

Walking times: Vila Nova – Coroa do Pico 1 hour, Coroa do Pico – start of the narrow path 1 hour, descent to Canto da Carneira ½ hour, ascent from Canto da Carneira ¾ hour, start of the gravel road – Vila Nova 1¾ hours. Total time 5 hours.

Height difference: 520m in ascent and descent.

Grade: easy walk. The descent to the Canto da Carneira is difficult since it goes on a steep and stony path (in places loose stones).

Refreshments: restaurants in Vila Nova.

Alternative: from the gravel road from Coroa do Pico small paths keep going through the walled gardens uphill left and downhill right. The paths uphill are less interesting, but take note of the paths downhill and possibly descend earlier to the coast.

Since most of the tourists come from Flores to Corvo by boat for just one day you can usually only find information about the trip to the caldeirão, but there are some beautiful places for watching birds and whales on the north-east coast which you can reach very easily. The path to Canto da Carneira is described here. A section of the walk is identical to the one to the caldeirão (see Walk 39).

The walk begins at the church in **Vila Nova do Corvo**. Go first of all up the narrow street out of the town. After two hairpin bends there's a section of road going up a gentle incline. Then, as previously described, the road goes across the Ribeira da Lapa and the Ribeira do Cerrado. When you come to **Coroa do Pico** on your right the path forks. The path to the left goes steeply up to the caldeirão and your path, a gravel track, continues right with a slight incline. Vegetable gardens and cornfields are on both sides so the path, below the road to the Espigãozinho viewpoint, goes to a height of 300m.

Now begins the adventurous bit. The path is narrow and covered in stones, and sometimes overgrown with grass, so that you need to be careful where you are putting your feet, especially since it is steep. The path descends very narrowly between the customary walls. The descent at the end is quite steep. You come to a small lighthouse on the right. Then you reach the coast near **Canto da Carneira**, a narrow stretch of beach at a small river where you can sit down and watch the birds and whales. Success cannot always be guaranteed, of course, but the chances are really good on this side of the island. The view of the steep coast and the glistening sea are very rewarding too.

Go **back** the same way.

Going to watch birds and whales on the north-east coast.

Index

A
Água de Alto 38, 40
Alem 59
Algar do Carvão 70
Angra do Heroísmo 68, 70
Anjos 62
Arrebentão 56
Arribanas 34
B
Barreiros 58, 59
Beira 94
Brasil 60
C
Cabeço das Cabras 78
Cabeço Gordo 106
Caldeira (Faial) 106, 108
Caldeira (Graciosa) 124
Caldeira de Cima 98
Caldeira do Inferno 113
Caldeirão (Corvo) 136
Calhau 84
Can Longa 124
Candelária 84
Canto da Areia 86
Canto do Caneira 138
Capelas 34
Capelinhos 116
Capelo 116
Casa do Guarda 108
Casteletes 96
Castelo Branco 114
Corao do Pico 138
Coroa do Pico 136
Corvo 134
Cruz do Bravo 108
Cruz dos Picos 54
D
Deserto de Faneco 62
Dores 122
E
Escola de Artesanato 86

Espigãozinho 136
F
Faial 104
Fajã de Caldeira 98
Fajã de São João 102
Fajã do Belo 98
Fajã do Centeio 94
Fajã do João Dias 94
Fajã do Tijolos 100
Fajã dos Bodes 102, 103
Fajã dos Cubres 98
Fajã dos Tijolos 98
Fajã dos Vimes 102
Fajã Grande 132
Fajãzinha 132
Farol de Rosais 90
Fazendas de Santa Cruz 128
Fenais 124
Flamengos 108
Flores 126
Fonte do Jordão 58
Forestry park Sete Fontes 90
Fort São Bras 60
Furna de Frei Matias 82
Furna do Enxofre 124
Furnas 44, 46
Furnas do Enxofre 70
G
Gaivotas 39, 40
Ginetes 28
Graciosa 118
H
Horta 108, 112
L
Lagoa Azul 30, 32
Lagoa das Furnas 44
Lagoa do Fogo 38, 40
Lagoa Secca 46
Lagoa Verde 30
Lajedo 130
Lighthouse at Farol de Rosais 90

Lombadas 36
Lombega 114
Loural 102

M

Madalena 82, 84
Malbusca 58
Manadas 96
Miradouro Terra Alta 86
Monte 84, 128
Monte Ajuda 120
Monte Brasil 68
Monte da Guia 112
Mosteiro 130
Mosteiros 28, 32

N

Nossa Senhora da Ajuda 121
Nossa Senhora da Fátima 62
Nossa Senhora da Guia 113
Nossa Senhora da Paz 42
Nossa Senhora do Pilar 62

P

Panasco 58
Pico 74, 78
Pico Alto 54
Pico Barrosa 38
Pico das Camarinhas 28
Pico das Cruzinhas 69
Pico do Cedro 34
Pico do Facho 69
Pico do Gaspar 46
Pico Pequeno 78
Pocinho 84
Ponta de Castelo Branco 114
Ponta Delgada 26
Ponta do Escalvado 28
Porto Pim 113
Praia 38, 40, 58, 60

Praia (Graciosa) 124
Prainha 86

R

Relvão 69
Ribeira da Badanela 128
Ribeira Grande 36, 38
Ribeirinho 93
Rocha dos Bordoes 130
Rosais 90, 92, 94
Rossio 120

S

Santa Bárbara 54, 56, 97
Santa Cruz da Graciosa 120, 122
Santa Cruz das Flores 128
Santa Maria 50
Santo Amaro 86
São Jorge 88
São Lourenço 56
São Miguel 22
São Pedro 92
Serroa 92
Sete Cidades 30, 32
Sete Fontes 90

T

Terceira 64
Terra-Nostra-park 46
Terreiros 96
Touril 60

U

Urzelina 96

V

Vale Formoso 116
Velas 92, 94
Vila do Porto 60
Vila Franca do Campo 42
Vila Nova do Corvo 136, 138
Vista do Rei 30